F*CK YOUR RESUME

F*CK YOUR RESUME

THE REVOLUTIONARY GUIDE TO

GETTING HIRED IN THE DIGITAL AGE

JEREMY DILLAHUNT

SONOMA
PRESS

CONTENTS

INTRODUCTION

SERIOUSLY, FUCK YOUR RESUME. Type "books about finding a job" into Amazon's search bar, and you'll find more than 4,000 results. The common trope is to begin by saying it's a whole new world out there, that the Internet changed everything, and that the old rules no longer apply. But despite the new landscape, people still use the same old map, rehashing job-getting strategies that are frozen in amber: network, be confident, stand out, find your purpose, and, of course, *update your fucking resume.* Even the best-selling guides fall prey to the same old formula—whether they're updated for "Web 2.0" or not.

If it really is a whole new world out there, then why are job experts paying little more than lip service to the most transformational evolution of the job market since the industrial revolution? Stuffing a single chapter on the Internet into tomes filled with 40-year-old advice is a bit like putting a new stereo into a busted-out Oldsmobile—yeah, there's something new inside, but it's not going to get you anywhere.

The Internet really has changed the landscape of recruiting and job seeking—and not in a way that any afterthought can clarify. In this book, we'll take a deep dive into how the game of getting hired has changed, as well as how you can use these changes to your advantage. Getting a job is no longer about having a shiny resume—because everyone already has that. It's about carefully cultivating a professional online presence. It's about being a true professional, online and off. It's about making the right connections. Do this, and jobs will more than likely come to you. And even if they don't—even if you find yourself having to send out applications—all the tools and info you need to pitch yourself as the ideal candidate will be right there at your fingertips.

New Landscape, New Rules

The first thing to understand is that hiring has become a numbers game. There are just too many job openings, new hires, and people on the hunt for it to be anything else.

According to the Bureau of Labor Statistics, there are, on average, nearly 15,000 job openings per day in the United States, or more than five million job opportunities per year. As with many other economies of scale, hiring has developed "efficiencies," a.k.a. software, to help manage a huge volume of work while bringing costs down. Software programs don't need sleep, don't take breaks, don't ask for raises, and cost whatever going rate the electricity companies are charging—plus Rackspace and licensing fees. In the same amount of time a human can pick up one resume, browse it for relevance, and decide whether to round file it or pass it along, a software program can do the same for hundreds.

All of this is to say that the numbers are not exactly in your favor.

Thick, stock, paper resumes and gimmicks to draw attention to yourself may have worked in the past, but a computer program doesn't care how clever you are or how nicely formatted your bulleted list might be. Rather than cast your lot with folks offering pre-Internet advice, you're better off getting a handle on how today's process works, what rules the software programs that comb over your application are triggered by, and why the hiring managers of companies big and small make the decisions they do. Once you know the rules of the game, you'll be much better suited to play it—and to make it through a process designed to filter out ill-suited applicants before identifying the good ones. The real business of getting hired increasingly takes place inside computer programs and behind the closed doors of personal referrals.

To thrive in this new landscape, you'll need to reorient your focus toward the evolving, digitized version of yourself that is accessible 24 hours a day, 7 days a week, 365 days a year: online you.

The Best You *You Can Be*

With the rise of LinkedIn and other online services, the people doing the hiring have a veritable ocean of information—about you and about anyone else that may be a good candidate—just a few key-strokes away. Think of it this way: A resume is a one-dimensional, black-and-white distillation of all the stuff you've done. Your online profile, in contrast, is a full-color, multimedia, high-definition version of *you*—your personality, job history, sense of humor, physical description, preferences, personal history, and creative and philan-thropic exploits. A resume doesn't stand a fighting chance.

Don't be mistaken: This book is not just for college graduates or those seeking their first job. The current work environment is con-stantly in flux; unless you're the pope or a supreme court justice, there's really no such thing as rock-solid job security, and you should always have an eye toward your next position.

How do I know? Because I'm no different than you or anybody else. Over the past 28 years, I've picked cherries, mowed lawns, sold popcorn at the movies, washed dishes, served food, cooked in a truck-stop diner, burned the leftovers of clear cuts, made backpacks, rode a bike, tended bar, moved boxes, carried coffee, edited magazines, writ-ten stories, licensed music, marketed financial products, developed events programs, played records, interviewed celebrities, and forgot-ten more things than I remember as ways to make money. And I'm not the exception to the rule. It is safe to assume that you—and most everyone else—will have a lot of different jobs during your lifetime.

Regardless of how many positions you hold, a long, successful career depends on developing a bulletproof skill set and a stellar reputation so you can get hired over and over again. The Internet is everywhere, and it never goes away. In the coming chapters, we'll look at how to use that permanence and ubiquity to your job-seeking advantage. No matter where you find yourself in your professional life, this book will be an invaluable tool as you work toward landing your next job in the brave new economy.

CHAPTER ONE

WHAT'S SO REVOLUTIONARY?

READING TIME ⏳ 20–30 MINUTES

The Numbers

What's so revolutionary about using the Internet to get a job? Most people already look for jobs and apply online. But that's just the tip of the iceberg. The real advantages lie underwater, so to speak. The revolution begins when you take the plunge.

It comes down to numbers. In 2015, there were about 60 million job openings in the United States. Thanks to the Internet, almost all of them are accessible by you, the job seeker.

Think about it this way: About 20 years ago, the only ways you could find a job were through word-of-mouth or the local newspaper. At most, you'd find maybe 1,000 jobs printed in the paper—and that would be a sizable want-ads section. And your personal connections? They might lead you to a dozen employers.

Would you rather connect with 60,000 times as many opportunities? Then you're going to need . . . the Internet. That 60x difference in scale is truly a big deal in the evolution of hiring.

Gatekeepers

It's not just the Internet's scale that makes it so essential to your job search. The Internet is also a critical tool used by hiring professionals: recruiters, hiring managers, and resource managers. Considering it takes an average of 37 days, according to the Bureau of Labor Statistics, to fill a position, and Workopolis.com notes that each position generally receives about 120 applications, that's . . . well let's just say it's a lot of work for someone to stay on top.

Those "someones," increasingly, are recruiters and hiring managers, the gatekeepers of the majority of jobs in the country. If you want to get hired, you need to know how they work, what tools they use, and—just as important as why they choose to hire a certain candidate—why they choose *not* to hire certain candidates.

The immense volume of jobs sloshing around the Internet can only be managed with the aid of . . . the Internet. Recruiters and hiring managers spend most of their time looking for candidates through services and channels such as LinkedIn and TheMuse.com. To get their attention, you'll need to be on the same services and channels— and understand what they're looking for.

The Professionals

RECRUITER	HIRING MANAGER	HUMAN RESOURCES (HR)
Recruiters are generally services that exist outside of the company that's doing the hiring. For example, Coca-Cola would hire XYZ Recruiters to provide it with a list of suitable candidates for a job it needs to fill.	Hiring managers work for the company that's doing the hiring. They will discuss resource needs with the various departments of their company and coordinate the various stages of finding the right person for the opening.	Human resources is often incorrectly used to describe those responsible for hiring. But that's not what they do. HR covers far more than hiring, and sometimes has nothing more to do with finding new talent than welcoming them to their new job.

What Are the Most Important Elements of Your Job Search?

Rank the following in order of how likely they'll influence the outcome of your search, with 1 playing the biggest role and 10 the smallest:

_____ Personal appearance		_____ Social media presence
_____ Interview		_____ Online profile
_____ References		_____ Recommendations
_____ Resume		_____ Suitability
_____ Work history		_____ Experience

If you put your resume in the top 7, you're not on the same page as most recruiters and hiring managers. For them, a resume is like the fine print—it needs to be there, but they don't need to read it every time. It ticks a box on their checklist, but it doesn't do much else. At best, resumes are perceived as an incomplete picture; at worst, they're disingenuous. "Most people list a bunch of stuff they've done, but that doesn't tell me as much as your LinkedIn profile can," notes Ryan Woodring, Director of Project Management & Creative Services at John McNeil Studio. "And besides, everyone lies on their resume. I mean, I've lied on my resume, so I know you're probably lying too."

Even so, many job seekers still think that their resume is an essential part of their search. Where's the disconnect?

For starters, most books about getting a job start with resumes. They're part of a widely accepted, out-of-date perspective on how to get hired. And sure, resumes did used to play a significant role in the job-search process, but that had more to do with the technical limitations and cultural etiquette of the time than their intrinsic utility.

Back in the Old Days

So, how did people used to go about getting a job? Laboriously. From the 1950s until the turn of the century, job postings were placed in the newspaper. People looking for work would pore over hundreds of 1-inch by 2-inch descriptions, day after day, until they found something suitable. (Classified ads were a newspaper's most reliable source of income. For their size, classifieds were the most expensive kind of ad to buy.)

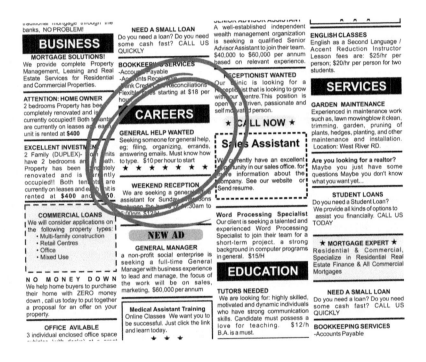

Since society was less mobile in the mid-20th century, most job postings were local. If you applied for a job, it was expected that you'd show up in person as part of the application process. You would also be expected to bring your resume, a cover letter, and either a letter of recommendation from a former employer or a testament to your good character signed by a notable person in the community.

So, to summarize, the application process involved:

1. Waiting for the daily newspaper to be delivered.
2. Searching through hundreds of relevant and irrelevant two-sentence job descriptions.
3. Obtaining past-employer recommendations or testamentary letters from a person of note.
4. Mailing hard copies of your resume, letters of recommendation, and cover letters—or, better yet, hand-delivering them.
5. Waiting for the prospective employer to respond, by mail, to your application.
6. Traveling to see your prospective employer for an interview.
7. Waiting for a letter confirming or denying your employment.

The process crept along at the pace of the US Postal Service. If you didn't like it, there was one other way to get hired: nepotism.

Handshake Hires

If you were looking for work in America after WWII, you would have gotten a leg up if you could take advantage of the "Old Boys' Club," a catchall phrase denoting the privileges of white, male, middle-to-upper class society. As long as you met those criteria, membership was unofficial, fairly loose, and self-reinforcing. But the benefits were enviable. Social networks were more tightly knit, and because of this many people in your own network would know when you were ready to enter the workforce. When the time came to get a job—an 18th birthday, for example—room was made for you within the professional connections of your social network.

Depending on your family's social stature or where you attended university, these networks could be expanded by orders of magnitude. A degree from an Ivy League school, for example, gained you entry into the offices of all the other graduates of that college. Additionally, gentlemen's clubs such as The Metropolitan Club of New York and The University Club of New York served as gathering places where social bonds could be formed. In effect, family membership in clubs and degrees from universities acted as passports to professional networks that would have otherwise excluded you. In many cases, these connections were all you needed to get a position at a law firm, hospital, or bank. Talent, skill, and performance were secondary to "character considerations"—where you went to college and who your family was.

As the 20th century moved on, merit, skill, and talent grew in importance and began to rival family connections and university degrees. This was partly due to work becoming more specialized and requiring more specific abilities and skills: An options or futures trader needs more than just a respected family name to do his job well. Another turning point in the history of employment was the rise of the Internet.

Which Brings Us to . . .

Present-day employment seeking begins with the Internet. Since Monster.com entered the field of recruiting in 1999, the process of searching for work and getting hired has moved almost entirely online. The Old Boys' Club and nepotism still play a large role in the job market—more about that later—but they no longer dominate it. Resumes, interviews, and newspapers have been diminished, too. If you want to get hired and you don't have the personal connections to pave the way, you need to master . . . the Internet.

Are you getting the picture?

The Big Picture

To boil it down, the difference between getting a job 30 years ago and getting one today hinges on the Internet. People are more mobile and willing to uproot themselves than they were a few decades ago, and that gives employers a bigger pool of talent from which to draw. Cities like New York, San Francisco, Austin, and Seattle are home to hundreds of thousands of white-collar migrant workers, all participating in a revolving-door work cycle that can mean regular cross-country transitions. From an employer's perspective, a perfect candidate is far better than an acceptable candidate—even if it costs $10,000 to pay for a moving service.

To make yourself an attractive candidate in this brave new work environment, you'll need a few important things:

1. **A strong online presence, including a professional LinkedIn profile, as well as spotless accounts on other social media networks.** Online profiles are quickly replacing resumes for potential employers as a way to gauge what sort of employee you'll make.

2. **Job board accounts.** You've got to be where the recruiters and hiring managers are looking. Also, you can't beat an automated, passive job search.

3. **Flattering online-search results.** It's best to present yourself in the most professional way you can across all social media channels. Just google "fired because of social media post," and you'll find dozens of instances of an employee's off-the-clock behavior being the catalyst for job termination. (And, honestly, what might seem funny in private can appear anything but in the often context-less light of public scrutiny.)

4. **A clear idea of what you want to do.** Just like the Internet, nothing ever goes away in the hiring industry. Software programs like Taleo keep track of everyone who applies for a job, and hiring managers add notes and comments to interview files. In this environment, blacklists of sorts exist to help recruiters keep tabs on time-wasting candidates who apply for jobs they're unqualified for.

5. **A personal reference and notification network.** While the Old Boys' Clubs of yore are slowly but surely losing relevance, many jobs are still filled through personal references. In fact, some of the recruiters I talked to guessed as high as 85 percent. However tenuous or small your network is, it will be a great asset in finding a job. (More to come on building and leveraging your network later.)

6. **A strong interview: If you make it to in-person meetings, you're already in the final running.** At this stage, it's likely that all candidates are equal as far as their skills and experience are concerned. Employers are really looking to get a feel for you—or for a reason to pass you over.

Last, if some ghost of hiring processes past actually does require you to hand them a physical copy of a *fucking resume,* rest assured. Know that, with all the work you've put into building a glistening online presence, satisfying any hiring dinosaur's needs for a printed list of your professional achievements on macerated wood pulp is as easy as exporting your LinkedIn profile and clicking "print."

What Lies Ahead

Over the next 12 chapters, you're going to learn about the infrastructure behind the hiring process. You'll come to know how recruiters and hiring managers work together, what programs and platforms they use, and how those services inform hiring decisions. We'll look at ways to see what your online profile looks like from your prospective employer's point of view, what you can do to make your profile better, and how you can optimize search results to show you in the best light possible. Additionally, you'll hear from recruiters and hiring managers about what they look for in candidates, what the most common job-seeking mistakes are, and how you can grab the attention of folks in the hiring seat. Most important, you'll build an attractive online profile—one that you can leverage toward building a network of references that not only gets you your next job, but all the ones after it.

So let's get going; you're ready for the next step: learning how to get not just any job, but *your* job.

"Google, I promise to keep my pants on."
—MATTHEW EPSTEIN

Epstein didn't get the job he set out for, product marketing at Google, but he did get a great position at a San Francisco startup. His example of how to create a multiplatform pitch in order to get hired was one of the first of its kind and is still one of the most enjoyable to learn from. You can find Epstein's pitch on YouTube.

GET IT DONE

1. Join LinkedIn, Facebook, and Twitter if you haven't already. You don't need to perfect your profiles now—we'll cover that later—but they are an essential part of your strategy. *Time on task: about 20 minutes each, or 1 hour total.*

2. Look into local meetups related to the industry you want to work in or the job you'd like to move into. If there are no local groups, you can always join online discussion groups via LinkedIn, hunt down industry-specific websites, or sign up for webinars. *Time on task: 2–4 hrs.*

3. Pack your online profiles with as much relevant information about yourself and the industry you're courting as you can—but don't overdo it. Simply linking to articles isn't enough; you also need to encapsulate key takeaways and, when possible, contextualize their importance for prospective employers. *Time on task: 1 hr (as needed).*

4. Join at least five job boards. *Time on task: 1–2 hrs.*

Resources

42 Leading Social Networking Sites for Business

www.linkedin.com/pulse/42-leading-social-networking-sites -business-you-may-know-gottlieb

LinkedIn is so successful it can promote its potential rivals without fear of selling the ground out from underneath its feet. You'll find niche interests like Black Businesswomen Online, FledgeWing, Young Entrepreneur, and many others here.

Your Resume vs. Oblivion

www.wsj.com/articles/SB10001424052970204624204577178894 1034941330

This is a classic article outlining some of the software programs and standard hiring procedures that make resumes about as useful as metric crescent wrenches.

Western Civilization's Historical Guide to the Job Search

www.mindflash.com/wp-content/uploads/2011/10/111017
_westsidejobsearch_V1.png

This simple infographic covers the last 5,000 years of the job market. The takeaway is this: Don't lose heart; you're living in the best time of human history as far as work goes. At any other time, you'd most likely be a slave or serf.

Bureau of Labor Statistics

www.bls.gov

The BLS is the US repository of almost anything you need to know about work. You can drill down into it for what feels like an eternity and still not run out of stats—particularly useful for big-picture analysis when you're new to an industry.

Industry-Specific Job Boards

www.quintcareers.com/indres

As of writing, Quint Careers, the host website, had a great list of job boards posted by industry. You can search through sports-, tech-, legal-, science-, and architecture-related boards, as well as many other job-posting resources.

CHAPTER TWO

DON'T JUST GET A JOB — GET *YOUR* JOB

READING TIME ⏳ 30–40 MINUTES

Everyone Is Different

Everyone has a dream job while they're growing up: astronaut, cowgirl, particle physicist, ski instructor, firefighter, baseball player, and so on. While experience tends to guardrail far-fetched notions as we get older, we all start out, as the saying goes, looking at the stars. Even so, not everyone has the innate capabilities to satisfy their childhood aspirations. Genetics and environment combine to give you a unique set of abilities and opportunities. This is not to say that your dream job won't make you happy (it's a dream job, after all!). But, the endless, unsuccessful pursuit of something less than realistic can make you very unhappy. In other words, it's a good idea to start your job search by squaring your desires against your skills, circumstances, and resources.

Know Your Strengths

How do you identify your "strengths," as they like to say in the business world? Sometimes it's easy. If you're five feet four inches tall, chances are you're not going to be running triangles in the NBA. (Of course, if you're fast, smart, and have a nearly four-foot vertical leap, you may be an exception. Just ask five-foot-three Tyrone "Muggsy" Bogues, the shortest player in NBA history, who was so good he once blocked a shot by seven-foot Patrick Ewing.) It gets trickier when you move beyond fairly obvious physical limitations, into your psychological, social, and emotional characteristics—and everyone is different. To get a sense of your own professional strengths, as well as where you might fall on a career spectrum, consider the following questions:

1. **Can you work with other people?** By that I mean, are you comfortable having your ideas challenged and modified by other people's input?

   Yes. The whole corporate world is your oyster. According to Forbes.com, employers identify the ability to work as part of a team as their highest priority when considering newly graduated candidates and within the top three qualities of seasoned employees.

   No. You might be better suited to starting your own business or working in a field that respects individual creativity such as the arts, entrepreneurial pursuits, or entertainment.

2. **Are you an organized person?** Can you keep track of independent projects, unrelated deadlines, and the minutiae of pushing a goal through to completion? Equally as important, do you find this kind of juggling satisfying?

   Yes. You'd be great in a project management role. People who can keep complex projects and their various parts and players under control are highly valued.

   No. You might be better off mastering a specific skill that employers need. If you're really good at a particular something—say, coding—your organizational skills are less important.

3. **Do people often ask you to repeat yourself?** Do people have trouble understanding what you're trying to say?

   Yes. If you can't communicate your thoughts clearly, you should probably stay away from any job that involves writing or the exchange of ideas: marketing, PR, journalism, publishing, politics, academia, etc.

   No. Good communication skills are the basis of entire industries. If you've got them, they can help you immensely. In any industry, if you hope to work your way into leadership roles, a.k.a. corner-office positions, you must be able to explain goals and strategies clearly.

4. **Are you good with people?** Can you listen, see multiple sides of a story, be patient and nonjudgmental, and easily connect with people on a personal and professional level?

   Yes. People skills are a must, especially if you aren't a specialist. They open up a lot of possibilities for management roles and are essential for any sort of client- and public-facing roles, particularly sales.

   No. Work is an inherently social environment for about 99 percent of the jobs out there. Your career trajectory will be severely limited without decent people skills—unless, again, you are really good at something. If you're something of an introvert, consider investing a good amount of time into mastering a skill.

5. **Are you flexible?** Do you handle stress well?

   Yes. Industries such as marketing, stock trading, and media are notorious for their volatility. You really need to be able to roll with punches if you want to pursue any kind of career in such fields.

   No. Plenty of careers depend on risk management, a.k.a., conceiving a plan and controlling the environment where it is set into motion. So, if you like to have control over your projects, pick a field dependent on set processes and specific rules.

These questions cover some of the fundamentals that employers use to assess candidates, but are no means definitive or comprehensive. Consider them as examples. Use them to come up with more questions specific to your nature and character. Once you've thoughtfully and realistically answered these questions on your own, it's time to test your own answers against those of people who know you well.

Feeling Anxious? It's Human Nature.

Even picking a generalized area of professional interest can be fraught with anxiety and second-guessing. Take comfort in knowing that it's not just you; it's human nature. In *The Paradox of Choice,* psychologist Barry Schwartz notes, "As the number of options increases, the costs, in time and effort, of gathering the information needed to make a good choice also increase. The level of certainty people have about their choice decreases. And the anticipation that they will regret their choice increases."

While Schwartz was writing about the psychology of happiness related to consumer options, it is no less true in the realm of early career choices. A 2014 survey by the Ireland-based professional social networking platform Kloodle noted that as many as 70 percent of recent college graduates felt confused and unsure over what career path was right for them. According to *Forbes,* as many as 60 percent of college graduates cannot find work in their field of study. While college itself is a prerequisite to getting hired in some industries, it doesn't seem like a stretch to say that there's a disconnect between what you study in college and who will hire you after graduation.

A/B-Test Yourself

In marketing, there's one pretty useful exercise used to help determine which of two options will perform better: the A/B test. It can be as straightforward as giving one (A) a group of people one option, and (B) another, but similar, group of people a different option, and seeing which one is more popular. But the A/B test has uses beyond marketing and can help you more objectively assess your strengths.

Think of yourself as the A group. Now, think of a combination of friends, family, peers, teachers, and past employers as the B group. Ask the B group the same set of questions you asked yourself, and you'll get valuable insight into your strengths, as well as what sort of career you may thrive in. Of all the people you could talk to, former employers will probably give you the fairest, least prejudiced assessment since they've seen your work ethic and decision-making process in action. No matter who you ask, getting a second (or third, or fourth) opinion can't hurt anything.

For example, you might believe you handle stress well. But if most people you know say the opposite, you should probably take their point of view into consideration before jumping into a role as a firefighter, rated the most stressful occupation of 2015 according to CareerCast.com. Or, just as likely, if you get a bunch of positive reinforcement regarding your strengths, you'll feel a boost of confidence before your job search begins.

But, what do you do if, after thinking through positions that might suit you, you still come up empty-handed? Honestly, very few people know what they want to do right off the bat. For instance, when I graduated college, I put in time flipping omelets, burning steaks, and stirring chili in a Montana truck-stop diner; cutting out backpack patterns; and fixing toilets, barstools, and decrepit air conditioners at a bar in New York before inching toward marketing and writing gigs. So don't worry; if you haven't figured out the exact coordinates of your career launch pad, you're not alone.

A/B Test

Ask three of your peers whether they agree or disagree that the following skills are among your core strengths.

	PEER 1		PEER 2		PEER 3	
	AGREE	DISAGREE	AGREE	DISAGREE	AGREE	DISAGREE
1: Teamwork						
2: Organization						
3: Communication						
4: Stress						
5: Interpersonal						

Results: If you get at least two agreements on a question, you're probably right. If not, you should probably reconsider what your strengths are.

Still, it is a good idea to know the general field you may want to focus on. The great thing is that pretty much every industry starts with a broad range of opportunities before narrowing down into more specialized roles as you climb the career ladder. So, if you see your future self as the Dean of Students at UC Berkeley, all you need to know right now is that an entry-level position in higher education is a good place to begin.

Don't BS Yourself

So, what to do? Ignore the stats and go after your dream job—but do it pragmatically. The old saying that, "In America, anything is possible," is mostly true, but it helps to consider "anything" through the lens of realistic, critical thinking.

Start by honestly asking yourself if you have, to cite the old cliché, "a passion" that you can see yourself dedicating the rest of your life to learning and perfecting. Don't worry if the answer is no. For most people, work is just work. It's not, nor should it be, the thing that constitutes their truest selves.

> "The law of work seems unfair, but nothing can change it; the more enjoyment you get out of your work, the more money you will make."
> —MARK TWAIN

Psychologist J. Anderson Thomson has written extensively on the gap between who people feel they should be and how they experience their present selves—who they actually are. Though most people don't have a clear idea of what sort of career is right for them, the idea that there is a "right" job and they just haven't found it yet can be somewhat depressing.

On the flip side, it turns out some folks enjoy their work the longer they do it. Psychologist Daniel Kahneman found that, the longer people stayed in a vocation, the greater their job satisfaction grew. In other words, the longer you do a job, the better you get at it—and that proficiency leads to enjoying your work.

If work won't make you happy, you can always retrofit work to allow you to pursue the things that do make you happy: travel, family, friendships, free time, buying lots of stuff, or whatever satisfies your desires. This is where being honest with yourself early in your career choices can pay dividends for the rest of your life.

Work to Live, or Live to Work?

I have a friend whose father enjoyed a stellar career managing one of the world's most recognized sports teams. Growing up in the shadow of a role model that enjoyed professional, personal, and economic success unrealized by most people on the planet, my friend naturally thought he wanted the same for himself.

He spent the better part of two decades working 70-plus-hour weeks, climbing the ladder of an early, groundbreaking tech company based in New York City. He could see his career future as clearly as if it was plotted on Google maps. And then, one day, he went to a party in Detroit, met a bunch of people who spent most of their time creating cool, if not salable, stuff, and packed it all in. Now, he's an abstract painter. He told me that he felt like he was suffering from a madness before he started painting. He works only as much as he needs to for rent, food, and painting supplies, and he's "never been happier."

Though likely less dramatic than the choice between tech stud or abstract painter, this is ultimately the choice that lies before you: recognize what the cosmos put you on earth to do and spend the rest of your life mastering it, or find a job (or several jobs) that will let you live the life you want to lead.

To help you figure out where you fit, I've ginned up an admittedly non–peer-reviewed worksheet. To use it, check the boxes next to the statements you feel best represent your own attitudes about work.

If you're mostly marking the right-hand column, you may want to look for satisfaction in life outside of work. If you're finding the

Career Paths

LIVE TO WORK	WORK TO LIVE
I know exactly what I want to spend the next 40+ years of my life doing.	All job options are equally attractive.
I'm comfortable being around people I don't know all the time.	I need deep, meaningful relationships with the people I'm around.
I'm very confident I know what I'm doing.	I second-guess decisions I've made all the time.
Offices are like second homes.	Offices make me uncomfortable.
Experiencing life through a specific filter is attractive.	The world is too interesting to narrow it down to one filter.
Knowledge for its own sake is useless.	I love learning for the sake of learning.
That my fate lies in other people's hands does not worry me.	I need to be in control of my own decisions and actions.
I dream about solving work-related problems.	When I think about my life, work is the last thing that pops to mind.
Work is its own reward.	I better get rewarded for this work.

opposite results, however, congratulations, you're on the road to a long, and no doubt fruitful, career in whatever your pleasure may be.

Still, it's important to remember that things can change. You may not be attracted to the idea of a career-focused life right this second, simply because you've yet to discover something that really excites your professional interests. Or, you may walk out of your office 30 years into your career and never look back. As they say, it's important to keep an open mind.

Rejection Sucks. Get Used to It.

Don't be discouraged if your first job application is rejected, or, more likely, if you never hear back from your first prospective employer—or your second, third, fourth, or fifth. Finding any job takes a long time; finding a job that's a great fit for you is going to take even longer. To put things in perspective, here's a story you may have heard a thousand times over: *The Guardian* noted that *Zen and the Art of Motorcycle Maintenance,* a book that ultimately went on to sell more than five million copies worldwide, was rejected by *121* publishers before anyone thought it worth the public's time. That's a whole lot of "nos" before even one "yes."

Carl Sweet, Marketo's Director of Talent Acquisition, recently put some time into figuring out the most efficient ratio of applications to interviews to hires. Looking at years' worth of data, Sweet analyzed hundreds of instances from when a job was posted to when it was filled. He found that the more complex and specialized the position, the fewer candidates a hiring manager would need to look at. But, when hiring multiple positions responsible for the same kind of work, resource directors needed to widen their search exponentially to net a core pool of good candidates. Here are some of his findings:

To put your job search in perspective, hiring managers first sift through profiles of candidates a software program has pre-selected for them. Once they have a solid pool, they'll conduct phone interviews to further narrow the field. Then come in-person interviews, and sometimes follow-up interviews with team members

Tech companies	Financial services	Engineers
80 CANDIDATES	125 CANDIDATES	20 CANDIDATES

8 INTERVIEWS   15 INTERVIEWS   5 INTERVIEWS

1 HIRE   1 HIRE   1 HIRE

the prospective candidate would be working with. Using Sweet's numbers for the Tech Industry, here's how much time a hiring manager could devote to filling a position:

- ▶ 80 phone interviews at 30 minutes each: 40 hours
- ▶ 8 in-person interviews: 8 hours
- ▶ 3 final candidates conducting 30-minute interviews with 3 team members: 4.5 hours
- ▶ *Total:* 52.5 hours per position

All of this is to say, yes, rejection sucks. But most job applications—the overwhelming majority of them, in fact—end in rejection. It also happens to everyone. No matter how you slice it, getting hired takes a long time. Patience, perspective, and perseverance will all do you well, particularly when you're just getting started.

Do the Time

You can spend as much time as you want searching for a job. If you don't have one and your days are open, you should probably spend at least 35 to 40 hours per week searching. But, like most people, you probably have other commitments. To help you manage your workload and search for a new job, use the following matrix as a guideline for how much time you should commit to different areas of the job-search process.

In this chapter we looked at ways to identify the type of job that's right for you, as well as how long you should spend on various tasks and steps in that process. In the next chapter, we'll pick apart that most flawed of candidate-evaluating tools—the resume—and look at ways that we, together, in the name of all that is holy, can move past it.

The Soul-Crushing Reality

So, when it comes to landing a gig, what are you up against? Here's a short list of somewhat soul-crushing numbers about the reality of 21st-century job seeking.

▶ Between three and nine months: Average time it will take you to land your first job after graduation (Experience.com)

▶ 118: Average number of applications per job posting

▶ 20: Percentage of applicants to get an interview

▶ 50: Percentage of resumes never seen by a person (software programs screen them out)

▶ 80: Percentage of job openings that aren't advertised (InterviewSuccessFormula.com)

▶ 52 days : Average amount of time it takes to fill an open position

Keep in mind that these numbers are just averages and will vary by industry, your experience level, your salary requirements, and several other factors.

TASK	TIME SPENT
SEARCH How long you spend searching for appropriate positions will largely be determined by the kind of job you're looking for. That said, there are so many different services and boards posting openings that if it takes you longer than a few hours to find a position, you're probably doing something wrong.	2 to 3 hours per day
APPLY A lot of today's hiring managers use an online application system. The time spent on this task will depend on a few factors.	Online application system: No more than 1 hour. Cover letter: If required, no more than 1 hour. Resume: Exporting your LinkedIn profile should take very little time. If you find yourself needing to heavily revise your experience to fit a certain position, it's probably not a great fit.
NETWORK Networking is the most efficient way to land a job you want. Spend lots of time doing it, more than any other aspect of the job search.	As much as possible. (More on this later)
ONLINE PROFILE It doesn't take a whole lot to maintain an online profile. Just schedule part of your day as dedicated to following up on this.	No more than an hour per day

Total: Just searching and applying for a single job can easily take up to 5 hours of your day. When allotting time in your schedule, carve out a 4-hour chunk at the minimum to allow yourself enough time to get it right.

GET IT DONE

1. Before you start thinking about your dream job, spend some time identifying your skills and strengths. Write down what you think your strengths are and examples of how they've helped you. Matching your skills and strengths to a field is probably the single best thing you can do to identify potential career options. So think on it carefully and at length. ⬡ *Time on task: 1–8 hrs.*

2. Ask people who know you about your skills and strengths. Pick at least three people who know you in different ways: friends, peers, family, former employers, teachers, and so on. Schedule each for an hour interview. ⬡ *Time on task: 4 hrs minimum.*

3. After you've done your interviews, evaluate the feedback you receive. If necessary, reconsider your conclusions based on those discussions. If everyone you talk to agrees with you, great! However, if most people you talk to disagree, you have a choice to make: to double down in the face of resistance, to ignore their feedback and go ahead with your ideas about what's a good career for you, or reassess from the beginning. ⬡ *Time on task: 1–8 hrs.*

4. Think about what kind of person you are. Do you live to work, or do you work to live? The answer to this question will have a huge impact on your long-term job satisfaction, as well as your overall personal happiness. If you have a strong sense of what you want to spend the rest of your life doing, this will be easy. But, if dozens of careers seem equally attractive, it may take some time to weigh the pros and cons of each. ⬡ *Time on task: 1–5 hrs.*

Resources

"Quitting the Paint Factory: On the Virtues of Idleness."
Mark Slouka, *Harper's*. November 2004.
harpers.org/archive/2004/11/quitting-the-paint-factory/
Productivity is often seen as a moral virtue in America; it is the action that equates work with goodness. Slouka's classic essay explores the importance of relaxation, laziness, and, in the present vernacular, "down time." A must-read for anyone attracted to creative pursuits.

"Dear Hume," Hunter S. Thompson. *Letters of Note*,
Chronicle Books, May 2014.
In this letter to his friend, a young Thompson displays self-awareness far beyond his 20-something years. He makes a nearly impenetrable case that people have two choices as far as careers are concerned: passion and lifestyle. I wish someone had shared this with me when I was in my teens.

"Best Career for Me" Selector
www.selectsmart.com/topjobs.html#collegetoo
This interactive tool is broad in its approach to career selection, but its questions can be helpful in catalyzing a preference for work.

Personality Test: What Job Would Make You Happiest?
www.theguardian.com/lifeandstyle/2014/nov/11/-sp-questionnaire
-what-job-would-make-you-happiest
This *Guardian* interactive tool can be helpful in figuring out where your interests lie. Take it as a general indicator.

"In Praise of Idleness," Bertrand Russell. *Harper's*, October 1932.
harpers.org/archive/1932/10/in-praise-of-idleness/
Bertrand Russell critiques the notion that work is its own reward from a class perspective—he was British, after all. If you've never been completely settled with the idea that you should love work in and of itself, this essay will give you an invaluable perspective, as well as the vocabulary to help define your own relationship to jobs, work, and careers.

CHAPTER THREE

F*CK YOUR RESUME

READING TIME ⏳ 20–30 MINUTES

The Script

From what seems like time immemorial, the people who give out jobs—and the people who write about getting jobs—have held resumes up as an essential part of getting hired. The script, they'll tell you, is simple: Polish your resume. Write a good cover letter. Practice for canned interview questions by rehearsing your "five-year plan" and spinning your personal flaws into strengths, and you'll be decorating a new cubicle in no time. But the conventional wisdom displayed in books like *What Color Is Your Parachute?* and *Job Hunting for Dummies* far overplays the importance of 1950s formality. The game is changing. And while you're busy typing out bulleted lists of your professional accomplishments, someone else is nabbing your dream job out from under your nose.

The Medium Is Not the Message

The first thing to understand is that most job seekers still intimately tie the function of a resume (to get an interview) with its form (a bulleted work history). But if you focus more on a resume's purpose, you'll get a much better idea of what potential employers are looking for—namely, a reason they should talk to you, and what other, successful job-hunters are doing to get hired. Employers want creativity and initiative from their employees. As a job seeker, it's pretty hard to make the creativity case for yourself using a 5-century-old format.

So, what's the alternative? Here's a short list of what some people have done to get their foot in the door:

▶ Registered the .com domains of the CEOs of companies they wanted to work for and, good naturedly, threatened to redirect them to Justin Bieber's fan site.

▶ Identified that the last seven people to follow a Twitter user have their profile pictures show up in the right-hand corner of the user's profile; they then spelled out "Hire Us" in profile pictures that linked to their portfolios.

▶ Purchased the names of would-be employers via Google Ad Words and linked the results to a "Hire Me" message along with work examples and a personal website.

▶ Created cereal box, chocolate bar, coffee cup, and other unconventional "resumes" to get noticed.

How does your bulleted work history look now?

The Long, Boring History of the Resume

Why are resumes still such a big part of job-hunting advice? In short, culture, habit, and history. Many people have thought of resumes as the epicenter of the job-search process for so long that it's difficult to imagine a work environment without them.

One of the oldest surviving examples of a resume belongs to none other than Leonardo da Vinci. In a 1482 letter to Ludovico il Moro, the Duke of Milan, da Vinci attempts to gain employment by highlighting all of the skills he can bring to the Duke's court. The introduction alone makes it worth reading:

Most Illustrious Lord, Having now sufficiently considered the specimens of all those who proclaim themselves skilled contrivers of instruments of war, and that the invention and operation of the said instruments are nothing different from those in common use: I shall endeavor, without prejudice to anyone else, to explain myself to your Excellency, showing your Lordship my secret, and then offering them to your best pleasure and approbation to work with effect at opportune moments on all those things which, in part, shall be briefly noted below.

Da Vinci then goes on to list his engineering abilities concerning building bridges, draining swamps, destroying fortresses, constructing catapults, forging bronze statues, and designing elegant buildings, among other things.

The History of the Resume

A traveling Lord in England offers a handwritten letter of introduction to aquaintances and calls it his resume.

Resumes still include personal info like age, weight, height, marital status and even religion.

Resumes start to get beyond the dry facts and include things like outside interests and other info to help paint a fuller picture of the candidate.

The first VHS portfolios are recorded and used. Books on resume writing and career counseling get very popular.

By 1987 fax machines become the popular way to distribute resumes. Video conferencing gets used for interviews.

1500s 1940 1960 1980

1930 1950 1970

Resumes start to become popular and are used to help employers learn the basic facts of people.

They become a formality and they are now expected for most professions.

Digital typesetting and word processors help the resume to become more of a sales tool.

The IBM PC is introduced in 1983. Microsoft Word is released.

Adapted from Optimal Resume: admin.optimalresume.com/upload/ResourceFile_university _ResumeHistory.pdf

Internet and the
World Wide Web
go public in 1994.
Monster.com
goes live and
CareerBuilder is
founded.

Email popular for
sending resumes.
Electronic digital
portfolios are
introduced.

Linkedin
launched in
2003 and
Facebook
in 2004.

Social media
becomes key
networking
resource and
means for
screening.
Linkedin
takes lead for
employment.

The resume
objective goes
out and the
summary or
position state-
ment comes in.

Resumes
contain
social media
links and
become
shorter but
with added
multimedia,
visual
options and
modularity.

1995

2005

1990

2000

2010

The dot com
boom hits full
stride.

Interactive
resume websites
released.

Personal
branding goes
mainstream.
Keywords and
SEO become
important.

Video resumes
hit YouTube.

Virtual
portfolios
become
the rule,
resumes and
letters get
even more
focused.

Resumes were simply letters of introduction that could open the door to a longer, more detailed conversation between potential employers and employees. But, over time, they evolved into their current bland and soulless form—snippets of your work history on one scannable page. Even though world economies and marketplaces have evolved hundreds of times over the same period, a lot of people still go about hunting for jobs using 15th-century techniques.

How Your Resume Hurts You

A resume-focused approach to job-hunting wastes both your time and your potential employer's money. Trying to land a position by looking up job postings and sending in your CV and cover letter—the "shotgun" strategy, as career advice experts call it—is horribly inefficient. The average job seeker can expect to send out dozens, if not hundreds, of resumes by taking this approach. In theory, the more applications you make, the better your chances of getting hired should be. In reality, that's not really the case.

Hiring managers, HR departments, and recruiters use various software programs, such as Taleo, to keep track of who has applied for which jobs. This information is stored away, forever, and is easily accessible in just a few clicks. Beyond just logging who has applied for what, hiring managers can leave notes and comments about how an applicant's interview went or their general impressions of someone. Most important, it can ID serial applicants. "If your name comes up over and over as someone who's applying to jobs beyond their experience level, you'll get blacklisted," notes Ryan Woodring. "Everyone is busy and the worst impression you can give someone who holds your fate in their hands is you're a time-waster."

"Resumes serve a purpose but aren't good for telling you if someone's qualified," notes Joan Miller, a headhunter in the advertising industry for the past 16 years. "Advertising is a connected community

Worst Resumes Ever

The Internet is full of questionable to downright scary inclusions in a person's work history. Here are a few of the standouts—and not in a good way:

- "Incarcerated from November 17, 2006, to July 18, 2007, for sexual assault charges."

- "Bachelorette degree in computers."

- Reason for incarceration: "We stole a pig, but it was a really small pig."

- "Married, eight children. Prefer frequent travel."

- "It's best for employers that I not work with people."

- Given email: pornstardelight@*****.com

- "I'm excellent at debating various issues, as evidenced by the fact that I constantly win arguments with my girlfriend."

- "I finished 2nd place in my fourth-grade spelling bee."

- On interests: "Playing with my two dogs (They actually belong to my wife but I love the dogs more than my wife)."

- "I got laid in March." (Instead of "I got laid off in March.")

- "Work well with ethnics and people of a different race."

- "I'm one bad-ass bitch."

- "Skills: expert at not stealing :)"

- On hobbies: "Getting drunk every night down by the water, playing my guitar and smoking pot."

- "Prior experience: Meth dealer."

- "I like the anime Bleach and I can make tea and coffee."

- "Misdemeanor solicitation of sex—all charges dropped."

- "Marijuana dealer and nefarious dude."

- "Master of masturbation."

- "Villanova was too easy."

- "ESP."

- "Skills: Strong Work Ethic, Attention to Detail, Team Player, Self-Motivated, Attention to Detail."

- "I am great with the pubic."

- Job motivation: "To keep my parole officer from putting back me in jail."

- "Marital status: often. Children: various."

- "My dream job would be as a pro-fessional baseball player, but since I can't do that, I'll settle on being an accountant."

based on relationships. Agencies are founded on collaboration, so you've got to know the various roles and where your skills fit."

A 2013 CareerBuilder.com survey found that 75 percent of applicants didn't even get an acknowledgment that their resumes were received. That's a lot of effort for very little reward. While it might feel rude to not get a response when you send in an application, it's more likely just a symptom of the changing nature of the hiring process. The Internet has made it easier for people to search for jobs—and employers to find potential candidates. The problem is that there are almost 280 million people online in the United States, according to Internet Live Stats—and that makes for one seriously large pool of candidates.

Consider the following:

▶ 7.6 million people applied for 6,500 jobs at Starbucks in 2014.

▶ 1 million people responded to the 2,000 jobs Procter & Gamble posted in 2013.

▶ Google recently received 2 million applications for 7,000 open positions.

Given such huge numbers, it's no wonder that the first stage of the hiring process from the employer's perspective is not one of selection, but of *de*-selection—weeding out candidates who are unqualified for any number of reasons. From a bottom-line perspective, de-selection may be the most critical part of the hiring process, especially considering that it takes, according to Bersin.com, on average, 52 days and $4,000 to fill a single position.

The New Gatekeepers

To cope with a glut of applicants, companies invest in applicant tracking system (ATS) software or hire third-party service providers to handle the hiring process for them—with a price tag up to millions of dollars a year. Such an expense is essentially correcting an unnecessary, yet inescapable, reality of the present-day job market: people will apply for anything, whether they're qualified or not. In fact, as noted in the *Wall Street Journal*, almost 50 percent of applicants aren't qualified for the position being advertised. "I stopped looking at resumes as a way to tell if a candidate's qualified or not pretty quickly," notes Joan Miller, a headhunter in advertising for the past 16 years. "More than half of them are applying for the wrong job and most of the rest are stretching their experience."

ATS plays a huge factor in whether or not a human being ever even reads your application. Such systems are not contextual; they can't look at the entirety of your work history and infer whether or not you're worthy of reaching the next phase of the hiring process. Rather, they scan for keywords, location, and other hard data

Top 10 Reasons Your Resume Doesn't Matter

Hiring managers and recruiters cite dozens of reasons why resumes are all but dead. Here are the big ones:

1. You're probably lying, at least a little bit.

2. They say nothing about whether or not you'll be a good fit for the company.

3. You can't explain gaps in work history.

4. Expertise can't be distilled into just a few words.

5. They provide little detail and no context.

6. They're prone to bias.

7. They're formulaic.

8. They're static.

9. You can't tell a story with a resume.

10. It's all about you.*

---

* Several recruiters have told me that candidates all too often make the hiring process about themselves. As far as employers are concerned, everything about you beyond your ability to positively impact their business is just a cherry on top. What can you bring to the table that will increase an employer's bottom line, save money, make a process easier, attract clients, or solve problems? Beyond that, it's all just unnecessary information.

points. And if they don't find matches, your application will end up in digital oblivion.

For example, an ATS may be programmed to look for "New York City," "copy writer," and "presentation" as filters for a NYC-based creative marketing job that requires sales experience. You might have the experience and be just across the Hudson in New Jersey, but without the exact words in your resume, your application won't make it past the first stage. To further complicate matters, keywording has become such a common practice that ATS programs are beginning to fail in their main duty. To bypass the software's noncontextual parameters, sometimes all you have to do is pull a few words out of the job-posting description and include them in your resume or cover letter.

What's more, some ATS programs have become so ineffective that hiring reps have been known to simply reject all applications submitted through them as a matter of course. Instead, they do their own searching on services such as LinkedIn. Most often, recruiters also function as a filtering layer and kick only the leftover applications to the person making the decision, the hiring manager. And how many resumes do hiring managers actually look at? According to the *Wall Street Journal*, only 19 percent look at the majority of applications, while 47 percent just consider "a few."

Many companies are even rolling back the high-tech approach in favor of the tried-and-true practice of asking current employees for referrals—which at least partially explains why 75 percent of all applications aren't even acknowledged as having been received.

Not the Real You

While resumes are mostly about your work experience, they are also about you. And while it's illegal to discriminate based on age, gender, or race, it still happens all the time; your resume will reveal all of those things, and more, very early in the hiring process.

"Be a Person. Not a Resume."

— SHARAD VIVEK SAGAR

According to the American Association of Retired Persons (AARP), it takes a person older than 55 three times as long to find a job as it does someone under 55. Additionally, the National Bureau of Economic Research found that applicants with white-sounding names received one callback for every 10 resumes submitted, while applicants with black-sounding names needed to send out 15 applications to get the same results. Discrimination can be overt, but it can also be a process of unconscious bias and personal experience. How many times in your life have you heard someone say they don't like a particular name? Or college? Or state? Or even something as simple as a word choice? If the very first phase of the hiring process is dependent on filtering out an overabundance of applications, any excuse, no matter how insignificant, will suffice for the time-strapped recruiter.

Consider your life: who you are, all of the love, hope, frustration, humor, and uniqueness that make up you. Now look at your resume. Big disconnect, right? A resume essentially blows something like 0.001 percent of your life—the things you do for money, to feed yourself and meet other material needs—out of proportion. By its very nature, the resume format excludes 99.009 percent of who you really are.

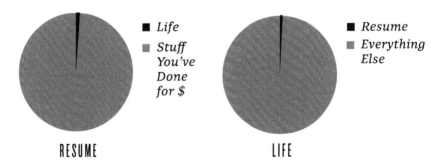

■ Life
▨ Stuff You've Done for $

■ Resume
▨ Everything Else

RESUME   LIFE

Destroy Your Resume

So, what are we to do with this inefficient, ineffective, and tedious holdover from bygone eras? Trash it! Use it to make a papier-mâché mask—a poetic statement about how your resume has been covering up your true self. Wrap your week's catch of fish in it. Or have your pals over for a good old-fashioned bonfire. Whatever you need to do to make shedding bullets of you in black and white cathartic, do that. Just be sure to hang onto some reasonably orderly record of your professional accomplishments; it'll make populating your online profiles that much easier.

While you've rightly moved beyond the resume, large swathes of the job marketplace have invested huge amounts of time and money building infrastructure, processes, and platforms that all hinge on resumes. Your goal is to make that silly sheet of paper what most recruiters and hiring managers already treat it as anyway—an extraneous part of the hiring process. To do so, you're going to buck the conventional trends and pathways of job hunting in favor of building an online presence that shows and tells who you are—and makes hiring you a priority.

Career-advice experts, HR reps, recruiters, and hiring managers are all counseling prospective employees to use various job boards and professional networks to research opportunities rather than to apply for positions. In an article for Forbes.com, Liz Ryan, CEO of Human Workplace, notes that dropping your resume in place of a career history and pain letter—a substitute for a cover letter where you research a problem the company is having and present a solution—results in a call back 25 percent of the time, partly due to the novelty of the format. Instead of listing a bunch of bulleted verbs ("Integrated a sales platform," "Increased revenue," etc.), you actually tell a narrative story about your work history.

Now, making the clean break from thinking about your resume as the cornerstone of your professional persona doesn't mean you get to be a slob. In fact, crafting a meaningful and memorable online presence requires at least as much attention to detail as formatting many series of bulleted lists. Getting sloppy and being careless can come

Career History vs. Resume

There are many ways to tell a story. When it comes to spinning a yarn around their work history, most people find themselves stuck in the resume rut. Here's an example of a way to share interesting, relevant, and rich information in the same amount of space a standard slugfest takes up.

RESUME

Managing Editor/Music Editor, Toyota Scion: 2011–2012

- ► Developed content strategies to increase brand awareness and engagement

- ► Grew Scion's owned promotions audience to more than one million

- ► Created email capture and self-activated audience development programs

- ► Built a social media amplification and distribution infrastructure

- ► Produced text, image, interactive, and video content for digital, print, and live events

WORK HISTORY

Managing Editor/Music Editor, Toyota Scion: 2011–2012

Working for Toyota was one of the best times of my career. A small group of us were tasked with building an opt-in promotions program to build awareness about Scion's line of cars. We did this by partnering with DJs, bands, visual artists, interactive designers, and film producers to share their work via online and print channels, as well as live events. More than one million people joined our program without us spending a dime on media purchases.

back to bite you. For example, Google has a policy of rejecting any candidates that submit materials containing a misspelled word—no matter how compatible or qualified they may be. If you make a fairly common, everyday mistake, you're SOL as far as Google is concerned. While Google's policy is stricter than a lot of companies in that it's written into their manual, almost every HR rep, recruiter, and hiring manager does the same thing. So, do yourself a favor: closely read any communication or document before posting it or sending it to a prospective employer.

Cover Letter vs. Pain Letter

The biggest difference between a pain letter and a cover letter is that in the former, you research, identify, and describe a solution for an issue directly related to the employer's needs. In the latter, as you've seen and heard a quadrillion times over, it's me, me, me—a letter focused on your strongest strengths and impeccable work history. Here's an example intro for both.

COVER LETTER

To Whom It May Concern:

I am writing to you in response to the Managing Editor position at XYZ Magazine. I was referred to your organization by _____.

I have over a decade of writing and editing experience at the following periodicals _____. Though I have a wide range of contacts and knowledge, my strengths are in the financial services industry and equities marketplace. I am a nonpracticing, certified analyst, but my main interest is writing, not trading.

Thank you for taking the time to look over my résumé. I look forward to hearing from you shortly.

Sincerely,

John Smith

PAIN LETTER

To: Paul Libassio, Editor-in-Chief, XYZ Magazine

c/o Angela Ankers, Hiring Manager, XYZ Magazine

Congratulations on the ASME Award for best financial services reporting! It must feel great to receive recognition for all of your hard work. You must be very proud of your team for creating such a high-quality magazine.

Awards are often given scant attention, but in the present business environment, I think they can make a big difference in terms of whether a magazine survives or thrives. While I worked at ABC Magazine, we invested heavily in producing quality reporting. The results paid off when we won DEF Awards. The recognition couldn't have come at a better time; the launch of our digital platform had really eaten into our operating budget, and we were stretched thin.

I have a ton of respect for the work your team does and would love to chat with you about how I could support and improve your efforts. Please let me know if you're interested and when your schedule allows.

Thanks and keep up the good work.

All best,

John Smith

The irony of current hiring is that an overreliance on tech platforms has created a flood of candidates too large to handle. In response, hiring gatekeepers find themselves retreating and retrenching into the analog, terrestrial roots of recruitment by giving preference to referrals and standout communications—even in hard copy. Even so, don't think that the Internet doesn't have a place in the future of hiring. If you take one thing away from this chapter, let it be the fact that resumes are old, tired, and going the way of the dinosaur. They can do more harm than good and just aren't the best way to communicate who a person is to a potential employer.

While the plumbing of online job markets may be clogged with easy-to-fool software and tens of millions of (often unqualified) applicants sending out resumes for whatever opportunities hit the top of their search results, as a job seeker, you need to make sure your online profile is scrubbed, polished, and ready for inspection. In the next chapter, we'll start looking at ways to do just that.

GET IT DONE

1. Destroy your resume. That's right; light it up. Shred it. Line your pet rabbit's cage with it. Do whatever you need to do to break the cycle of boring. ☒ *Time on task: 0–2 hrs.*

2. Think about a better way to tell the story of your professional history. Spend some time crafting something of a work history as a resume stand-in—particularly for those employers who still require some semblance of one. ☒ *Time on task: 1–2 hrs.*

3. Do some research into a company with an open position you're considering. Practice writing a pain letter—a letter essentially offering a solution to a problem the company is dealing with. ☒ *Time on task: 1–2 hrs.*

Resources

How We Stopped Reviewing Resumes and Started Making Better Hires

www.fastcompany.com/3051257/lessons-learned
/how-we-stopped-reviewing-resumes-started-making-better-hires
This article from *Fast Company* details the extensive process that
Compose, a Silicon Valley coding firm founded by IBM, created to
identify, vet, interview, and hire employees. Almost none of it is based
around a resume.

25 Brilliantly Creative Resumes

www.creativebloq.com/career/creative-resumes-11121419#null
From purchasing Google Ad Words to pinning Google maps, resumes
have come a long way from simple one-sheet pieces of paper. If you're
still thinking that listing your work history, skills, and education is
enough to get you in the door, check out what your competition is doing.

How to Write Your First Pain Letter

www.forbes.com/sites/lizryan/2015/03/01/how-to-write-your
-first-pain-letter/
This piece from *Forbes* walks through the who, what, where, when,
why, and how of pain letters. If you're having trouble writing your
own, take some tips from the pros.

CHAPTER FOUR

... AND GO ONLINE INSTEAD

The Internet Rules

Getting hired is all about connecting with people. And there is no better way to connect with people than the Internet. At the time of this writing, there were 3,284,145,293 people using the Internet worldwide. But by the time I finished typing that sentence, there were 3,284,145,346 using it; the number of Internet users grows at about 10 people per second.

If you compare online platforms to IRL ones, it's not even close. The *Wall Street Journal* is the largest circulated newspaper in the United States at 2.4 million people. Facebook, on the other hand, reaches more than 150 million people in the United States every day. To put that number in perspective, the size of this period > . < is about ⅟₂₅th of an inch. If the width of the period represents the daily reach of the *Wall Street Journal*, Facebook's US daily reach would look like this:

WALL STREET JOURNAL

FACEBOOK

Now, consider the cost comparison of the *Wall Street Journal* ad versus a similar Facebook ad. Running a 1.68" × 2" career advertisement in the *Wall Street Journal* for two days will cost you $8,578.56. For the same amount of money, you could run a Facebook ad for 40 days.

You Get What You Pay For

There's another big difference between the services you're paying for. If you're an employer placing an ad in the *Wall Street Journal*, you are buying ad space. There's no guarantee that anyone will see it; you won't know if 100,000 people or 2 people actually noticed your posting on the career page—picking it out of the presumably dozens of others surrounding it.

Facebook, however, lets you choose how to spend your budget. You can spread your investment out over a few weeks or choose a per-view metric—meaning every time someone views your ad, a small portion of your budget is used. The real kicker is that Facebook tracks all of the activity associated with your ad. Not only can they show you how many people saw it and over what period of time, but they can also tell you which users clicked on it. That's just one of the many reasons why job searching and posting has moved almost entirely online.

Another big reason recruiters and employers have moved almost entirely online is the flexibility that comes with the medium. The old-school process of placing advertisements in newspapers and trade journals was time-consuming and rigid. First, a company or business would have to see if there was available space in the publication. Then they would negotiate the price, create the advertisement, send the content to the publishers, wait for it to be printed and distributed, rest while the subscriber and reader base browsed the want-ads section, and finally sift through the snail mail replies. All told, the whole process could take as long as a month just to get someone in the door for interviews. Additionally, the process could not be changed on the fly. A company that decided it needed to fill a research and development position instead of a business development one would have to start the process over from scratch—leading a lot of applicants on a merry trip to nowhere in the process.

Kelly Milner, founder of BettafishConnect, is a recruiter who finds talent for digital creative agencies. Here's how she describes her hiring process:

If you're on LinkedIn, it means you're a passive candidate—someone who's most likely open to being contacted by a recruiter. So, from my perspective, I'm not going to waste time posting a job, waiting for the responses to pour in and then sifting out the 90 percent who aren't qualified. I partner with the hiring manager to figure out who's the ideal candidate and consider the whole role—skills, design style, and personality.

I can find out all sorts of things about people through their social media, Google searches, LinkedIn Recruiter, and BooleanBlackBelt.com. There's a ton of tools for me to use. Maybe I'll spend six seconds on someone's profile, maybe a bit longer, but usually it's a really quick decision whether or not I'm going to pass over someone or reach out to them. Once I find a half-dozen to a dozen people that are good, I reach out to them. I need to find out their motivation: Are they happy where they are? Do they want to try something different? Is it just about money? Do they want more time at home? The days of keeping portfolios on file are over. I can get so much more online, and if you're not there, well, you've got no chance, because you're just making more work for me.

The Benefits (and Dangers) of Social Media

Social media gives employers an edge they didn't use to have: targeting. For example, a newspaper like the *Chicago Tribune* can reasonably claim to represent a geographic area. Even so, demographically, they are all over the place. The best description the *Tribune* might be able give of their audience is, "Men and women, generally aged 30 to 80, majority Caucasian, but also African American, Latino, and Asian. Politically speaking, it's a Democratic town, but we're also read by Republicans. Economically we appeal to people making between $40,000 and $5 million per year." In other words, pretty much anyone. To compensate for the lack of reader specificity, advertisers need to create ads for a narrow audience, which, in effect, alienates or does not appeal to all of the nontargeted readers.

LinkedIn, by comparison, provides potential employers with a huge database—396 million and growing—of self-identified candidates. Instead of casting a wide net over a huge area, hiring managers can deploy a targeted approach to finding the right person. For example, a Scottsdale, Arizona, insurance company could ask LinkedIn to place an ad in the feed of anyone meeting a set of specific criteria—say, lives within 60 miles, has more than 15 years of experience in sales, possesses a Rolodex of area businesses, and has a proven track record of building and managing teams.

Just as LinkedIn can be an invaluable tool for employers searching for candidates, it is also a few steps away from candidates' private lives via sites like Twitter, Facebook, and Instagram. While it's less common for employers to sift through these feeds for prospects, they do offer a good vetting opportunity. Someone might look fantastic on LinkedIn, but turn out to be less than stellar on Facebook. Many people have been fired from their jobs for posting racist or sexist comments or images, as well as evidence of illegal drug use and excessive drinking. According to EmploymentLawDaily.com, social media is quickly making its way into the legal system on a variety of issues from labor relations to background checks, class action motions, trade secrets, and first amendment issues. While there are real ethical and moral arguments to be made around whether or not it's your future employers' business what you do outside of work, the reality is that, in a system that provides a glut of candidates for employers, any reason that helps a hiring manager narrow the field is one they'll use. In short, don't post anything that could compromise your chances of getting hired (more on this later).

Why You Should Go Online

If you're not using job boards, social media, and professional recruiting services to help you search, you're missing out on the advantages that $72 billion worth of investment—how much US corporations spent in 2013 on recruiting services, staff, and products, according to Forbes.com—can bring you.

"If you don't have everything online—work history, examples, evidence of engagement—you'd better be the Leonardo da Vinci of what you do 'cause you're just making more work for me."
—RYAN WOODRING

Right now, as you read this, dozens of software programs are scouring more than 200 job-board sites, social media platforms, and anything and everything else relevant online. If you're not there, the software programs can't find you. Here's a short list of what these programs and services do for employers:

- ▶ Create advertisements and promotional materials
- ▶ Develop job requisitions
- ▶ Place and manage recruitment advertising and promotions
- ▶ Recruit at universities and colleges
- ▶ Provide relationship management programs
- ▶ Source key candidates for critical roles
- ▶ Screen and check references
- ▶ Create an interview process using video and other interview tools

- Train and engage hiring managers in the recruiting process
- Select and implement an applicant tracking system
- Create mobile career websites and experiences
- Support candidates through the interview process
- Hire and train recruiters
- Access third-party agencies and executive recruiters
- Measure the process, focusing on speed, quality of hire, and efficiency
- Onboard new people

Essentially, employers have built a massive infrastructure that does the work of finding your next job for you. But there's a catch: You have to be on the right sites and platforms in order to benefit. So don't wait; your dream job could have just passed you by.

Get Others to Do the Work for You

RECRUITERS

Professional recruiters are paid to get you a job. That is to say, it's their responsibility to sniff out the best candidates available for their clients' open positions. If you're looking for a job, developing relationships with staffing agencies, resource managers, and recruiters is a very, very good idea.

Recruiting companies have existing relationships with employers, will work for you while you're looking elsewhere for a job, and, in many cases, fill positions that are never made public. Additionally, they'll have dozens, if not hundreds, of jobs to fill at any given time and will keep your information on file, giving you both a larger number of compatible jobs available to you and a longer window of time in which you might make a match.

According to LinkedIn's Talent Blog, resource management has grown to be a $400-plus billion per-year industry over the last century. Just as most agencies specialize in a particular industry—banking, education, entertainment, tech, etc.—they also divide who they're searching for into a wide variety of segments, from experience to skill set to salary requirements. Finding recruiters that are right for your career path is essential; your search will be much more efficient if you focus on recruiters that are relevant to your skills and interests. Just as work has become more and more focused on specialized skills, so has the recruiting industry. That doesn't mean that agencies don't cross over in their focus; it just means that if you want to start a career in publishing, it doesn't make much sense to approach a financial services staffing firm.

Just as with a prospective employer, you'll want to present yourself as professionally as possible when you meet with recruiting agencies. For the most part, they get paid when they fill open positions and will not waste time on candidates they don't think their clients will hire. If you're just starting out, don't worry. You don't always have to know how to do the job to get it. Even so, it's not a bad idea to read up on the big-picture trends, recent events, and historical context of the industry you're targeting. In a zero-experience game, the candidate with more knowledge who shows more interest in the job will likely prevail over ones who haven't done their homework.

Last, many recent graduates skip working with agencies, thinking that since they're looking for their first job, recruiters won't be interested in them. *Don't do this.* Companies like GradStaff specialize in placing graduates with little to no experience. And remember, almost no employer expects entry-level hires to know what they're doing. Most companies treat such positions as paid training opportunities, which is why the salaries are so low.

JOB BOARDS

Another essential, non-resume tool you, as a job seeker, need to familiarize yourself with is the job board. Like many online services, job boards were developed as a more efficient version of newspaper classified ads. Since their inception, they have all but entirely replaced the classifieds. Job boards like Monster.com, Indeed.com, or CareerBuilder.com are similar to LinkedIn, minus the social aspect, in that companies and individuals use them to post available positions and research the experience and availability of people seeking to find a job or switch companies.

Probably the biggest benefit to joining job boards is that recruiters, companies, and resource agencies regularly "scrape" them. Using software programs that filter for keywords, demographics, experience, salary requirements, geographic location, and a host of other factors, staffing agencies will collect the profiles of promising candidates for available jobs and future openings. By joining job boards, you are essentially becoming a passive participant in a fully automated, 24-hour-a-day job-search service. If you're just starting out, consider joining

- ▶ CareerBuilder.com
- ▶ CollegeRecruiter.com
- ▶ Indeed.com
- ▶ Jobing.com
- ▶ LinkUp.com

- ▶ LiveCareer.com
- ▶ NetTemps.com
- ▶ SimplyHired.com
- ▶ US.jobs

As with recruiting agencies, job boards can also specialize in specific industries and skill sets, so it's a good idea to do some research and join specialized sites when you can. Generally speaking, specialized sites will give you a better chance of directly connecting with the people who are actually hiring for open positions, which brings you one step closer than recruiters will.

WHAT EXACTLY IS AN ONLINE PROFILE?

Using a variety of tools and services, you are going to create something of an online persona. For the vast majority of prospective employers, recruiters, and hiring managers, this will be the first time they interact with you—the very first version of you that they see. First impressions count, so make sure yours is a good one.

Put yourself in a hiring manager's shoes. Which source of information would you rather have access to when making a decision to hire someone?

An online profile is really just the collection of all the various expressions of self you are already building—via LinkedIn, Facebook, Google+, Instagram, Twitter, news stories, and anything else that goes into the Internet. Taken together, these platforms and services constitute the "online profile" that recruiters and employers refer to.

RESUME		ONLINE PROFILE
x	Work history	X
x	Education	X
x	Contact info	X
x	Skills	X
	Recommendations	X
	Work examples	X
	Blogs	X
	News coverage	X
	Twitter feed	X
	Hobbies	X
	Sense of humor	X
	Daily life	X
	Awards	X
	Certifications	X
	Professional memberships	X
	Volunteer work	X

Why they matter is simple: As noted in the *Huffington Post*, assuming you've made it past their keyword filters, 80 percent of employers will Google your name before inviting you to an interview. Those results will determine whether or not you move on to the next phase of the interview process.

You've got three possibilities facing you when Googled by a potential employer—and only one of them is good for you.

What Your Potential Employer Sees

POSSIBILITY 1	POSSIBILITY 2	POSSIBILITY 3
They find a picture of you spraying beer out of your mouth while diving headfirst into the ball pen of a kiddie play area at your local McDonald's. This is not a good look. If an employer sees anything remotely like this, your chances of getting hired are, to quote my Appalachian uncle Walter, "Shitcanned."	Nothing much comes up. You are a neutral online person, neither good nor bad. There's a link to your Facebook profile, Instagram account, and maybe a high school graduation notification from your hometown's local newspaper. The problem is that neutrality is negative in the job market. Being unremarkable does not cut it in a world of cut-throat online geniuses who know how to tilt Google results in their favor. They are your competition, and they are kicking your ass if your profile returns a picture of Caspar Milquetoast.	Bam! You're all over the place: Twitter, LinkedIn, Facebook, Pinterest, Google+, and Instagram. And not only are you all over the place, but also you're a really interesting, positive, and dynamic individual with lots to say and fun things to share with other people. This is the result you want. In an age of the curated self, the job market does not look favorably on those who aren't, to borrow a favorite technology phrase, "engaged."

So, whatever moral qualms you may have about purposefully generating a positive, interesting you for the benefit of potential employers, shelve them; we're living in a weird reality, and fighting it is like trying to stop the ocean from making waves.

Now go ahead and Google yourself. See who you are as far as the Internet is concerned. It doesn't matter what the results are now, because you can make them better.

Essential Platforms

Ginning Google results in your favor starts by setting up accounts and actively using a bunch of free, easy-to-use services.

GOOGLE+

Yup, no one knows what to do with Google+ yet, not even Google. But they've made it necessary for anyone trying to build an online profile to use. Why? Google+ posts will likely show up in your results when someone Googles you. Google+ is probably the fastest way for you to pepper your search results with things over which you have some control.

LINKEDIN

While there are imitators, LinkedIn really has no competition when it comes to creating an online profile that's specifically tailored to professional life. Your LinkedIn profile should be as spotless as the Queen of England's tea service. The best part about LinkedIn is that it's nearly idiot-proof to create a finished, mistake-free profile. Just follow the pop-up instructions that appear at every step of the process.

TWITTER

Let the people running it worry about answering questions like, "Is Twitter viable?" and "Will Twitter ever turn a profit?" All you need to know is that there are 307 million active monthly users on the platform. More important, Twitter is the de facto champion of making it look like you're hip to what's important to a prospective employer's business. Twitter is where everyone in business posts links to

To Blog or Not to Blog, That Is the Question

Nearly everyone in recruiting says that blogs are essential for career advance-ment. The problem is that blogs require commitment, diligence, and a real knack for saying something interesting. Unfortunately, the true purpose of most blogs seems to be marking the grave of their creators' initiative. I'll leave the blogging question up to you to decide. But if you do go for it, treat it exactly the same way as you would a puppy: with regular care and attention; otherwise, it'll just end up shitting all over your job chances. ▲

articles they haven't read, reports they haven't studied, and videos they stopped watching after 15 seconds, with taglines like, "Really good insight from #RichardBranson, worth the time." Share as many articles as you can about the industry you want to work in; people will think you're "#OnIt."

FACEBOOK

There's really no reason for any employer or recruiter to peep your Facebook page other than to find a reason not to hire you. Don't give them one by posting the beer spray picture, blathering on about politics, or swearing excessively. (Some people don't realize this, but it's really no different from potty mouthing on a public bus.) You want your Facebook page to scream, "Good, clean fun!" Boring, I know, but them's the breaks of the job marketplace.

INSTAGRAM

As with Facebook, there's really no reason for an employer or recruiter to seek out your presence on this platform. But, it's reasonable to assume that they will anyway.

PINTEREST

While places like LinkedIn and Twitter might do the most for rais-ing your online profile in the day-to-day, there's still a place for Pinterest. Consider using it to keep up with professionals in areas of professional interest or for showcasing some of your better work, particularly if you're in a creative field.

There Are Rules

So, the previous platforms are most essential, but, depending on the industries you're trying to court, you might also consider setting up and managing accounts on YouTube, Amazon, Yahoo!, My VisualCV, and more. They'll all likely show up in your Google results. But, whatever you do, make sure you follow these rules:

1. **No racism.** Seriously. So many people have been fired or rejected from jobs because they make a racist joke (not funny) or post a racist image (also terrible). You will have little to no future in the workplace if you're flying a racist flag.

2. **No sexism.** Cut and paste everything from *No racism* and put it here. You'd think this would be obvious, but even public officials say the darnedest things about women on a regular basis—and still manage to look shocked when they are forced to resign because of it. You're not a senator or a congressman, so you won't get a press conference to apologize and try to explain yourself. You'll just be fired or rejected.

3. **No violence.** No one likes a bully. Simple as that.

4. **No drugs.** While THC gummy bears may be legal in a handful of states, you will probably cut your prospects in a lot of the other states if you take to reviewing mellow candies or any other mind-altering substances online.

5. **Civilized drinking only.** It's safe to assume that no one has ever been fired for taking a picture holding a glass of pinot grigio at a yacht club. But, you can kiss your shot at a new desk goodbye if a recruiter happens upon pictures of you slamming Jäger bombs with your bros at Chili's.

6. **Consistency.** Whatever you say on your LinkedIn profile, make sure it echoes what you put on any of your other accounts. You can't be the "Director of Operations" on one site and "Assistant to the Flower Waterer" on another. If nothing else, consistency across multiple platforms will show prospective employers and recruiters that you have a handle on version control.

Some Things Never Change

Let's put a sock in the trumpet of revolution for a moment and pause to consider that human beings are naturally conservative, if not curious. While it's great that you've decided to give your resume the bird, you still need to treat actual humans the way you'd want to be treated. Here are a few standards you need to uphold during your job search—even online.

▶ **APPEARANCES MATTER.** You don't have to be the embodiment of sartorial progress in person or online, but you should be clean and sharp. Shave that growth on your face into some sort of intentional form and, remember, side-boob is only for hot-mess celebrities.

▶ **FOLLOW UP.** I mean, I can't believe I even have to write it down, but the number of times I heard, "You wouldn't believe the number of people who don't send a thank-you note," from hiring managers I interviewed makes me want to weep for the future of civilization.

▶ **BE POLITE.** In every communication you have with a prospective employer, whether in-person or online, you must be polite and good-natured. Never, ever disparage anyone or anything while looking for a job. Negativity will sink you faster than the *Titanic*.

▶ **HOLD YOUR TONGUE.** There's such a thing as being too friendly—as well as too transparent. You don't want to appear too familiar with anyone until a few months after you've been hired.

▶ **SAY IT LIKE YOU MEAN IT.** When all things are equal, the candidate who is enthusiastic will win out over the candidate who isn't. Even when you're retweeting, show some genuine interest for chrissake.

And that's about it. You'd think a lot of this would be self-evident—falling under the more general headings of "use common sense" and "don't be an asshole." But the media has created a dependable revenue-stream out of featuring stories like, "A local man was fired after posting a picture on his Facebook page. The photo appeared to show him in blackface, holding a leash tied around a woman's neck, while kicking a cat and smoking what appears to be marijuana out of an empty bottle of Jack Daniels."

Don't be "local man." In the next chapter, we'll talk about finding a voice and brand for yourself—before someone else does.

GET IT DONE

1. Google yourself. If you don't stand out from the crowd of everyone else sharing your name, you need to rectify that. *Time on task: 15–0 mins.*
2. Familiarize yourself with what Google+, LinkedIn, Twitter, Instagram, and Facebook are. *Time on task: 15–30 mins.*
3. Memorize the rules of sharing anything online. If you adhere to them, employers won't have any (non–work-related) reason not to hire you. *Time on task: 15–30 mins.*

Resources

BooleanBlackBelt.com

This blog is run by Glen Cathey, a supersmart dude who figured out how to get hyper-specific in his hiring searches by using a lot of math, software, and brain power. He's the big data guru of the recruiting world. Reading his entries will help you understand how "talent," a.k.a. you, is acquired.

LinkedIn Recruiter

www.business.linkedin.com/talent-solutions/recruiter
Recruiter is one of LinkedIn's products. It's not free, but you can be guaranteed that 99.99 percent of headhunters use it. Read about it, try the lite version, download the PDFs, take the demo, watch the video, and so on. Familiarizing yourself with the tools the recruiting industry uses is a really good idea.

Ask the Headhunter

www.corcodilos.com/blog
Nick Corcodilos is, probably more than anyone, giving the recruiting industry a good name through his blog. He answers questions, has years of experienced insight, and provides tons of content that applies to most every job-search scenario.

CHAPTER FIVE

BRAND YOURSELF (BEFORE SOMEONE ELSE DOES)

READING TIME ⧗ 35–45 MINUTES

Personal Branding—Not as Sleazy as It Sounds

In the old days, if you wanted to land a job, it was usually enough to be poised and confident and have some professional experience—or at the very least, the skills to do the job. Today, though, those qualities make up the bare minimum, and a lot of people have them. Like no other time before, people are connected with one another, opening windows into their personal and professional lives, all over the Internet. This new landscape means it's possible, even likely, that potential employers will form an idea about you as a person, and as an employee, long before they decide to meet you—assuming they ever do. How people perceive you—based largely on what, and how, you share online—can make or break a job opportunity before it even exists. For these reasons, personal branding is hugely important. Do it with care, and you can strike a positive tone with potential employers. Do it badly and you can come across as vain, egocentric, opportunistic, and inauthentic.

While you can't control how other people perceive you, you can influence outsider perception by being conscious and intentional about what you share. Besides, if you do nothing, you will be subjected to the analytical, decontextualized whims of Google's algorithms.

Bring More You to the Table

The conventional wisdom on building a personal brand has two main components. The first is tactical: identify your professional strengths and package them. The second is the conceptual component: intentionally construct the best version of your *self*. In the words of Catherine Kaputa, author of *You Are a Brand!*, "the trick to effective self-branding is to devise a strategy that works in achieving professional and life goals but is also true to you—that brings more of you into the equation."

First, let's understand the tactical component. Everyone you meet, in person or virtually, will perceive you in their own way. Their perception of you will largely depend on the circumstances and environment in which your meeting takes place. Absent mind-control powers, you can't really dictate how someone else perceives you; even Mother Teresa had haters. At best, you can put your best self forward and hope your efforts will be taken as you intended.

The conceptual component is a bit more slippery to grasp. It's about bringing some of the largely intangible you-ness that makes you unique into the profile you're trying to create. Beyond having the basics, like the necessary skills for a particular job, these intangibles can be the basis for shaping perception in the minds of outsiders— particularly potential employees and clients. While yes, a lot of getting hired has to do with being able to do the job, there's also a good portion of the process that has to do with expressing yourself as an individual.

Five Classic Roles You Can Build Your Brand Around

Genetic and biological diversity are a hallmark of human beings. Even so, businesses, corporations, and industries are at heart conservative, operating far more on existing, proven knowledge than untried strategies. All of this is to say that you're not completely on your own when it comes to shaping a personal brand. There are plenty of existing prototypes for you to use as the basis for building your own brand.

What follows are five classic workplace roles and their associated qualities. Pick one role that you feel best represents you (of course, the qualities are not exclusive to their associated role). You can use these qualities as touchstones of your personal brand by producing content that highlights and show-cases them.

LEADER	CREATIVE	QUALITY CONTROL	SALESMAN	MANAGER
Decisive	Inquisitive	Independent	Curious	Organized
Trustworthy	Progressive	Impartial	Modest	Disciplined
Fair	Observant	Credible	Focused	Adaptive
Confident	Challenging	Reliable	Uninhibited	Empathetic
Determined	Self-reliant	Intelligent	Patient	Frank

Where to Build Your Personal Brand

The "where" and "how" of building a personal brand is arguably the easiest part. You are going to create your personal brand online using the tools in your online profile. Each one presents a different facet of how to express your brand and offers different opportunities concerning your career. They are:

1. LinkedIn: 94 percent of recruiters actively use it
2. Twitter: 55 percent of recruiters actively use it
3. Your blog or personal website, if you have one
4. Facebook: 65 percent of recruiters actively use it (per the Capterra Talent Management blog)
5. Google+: 18 percent of recruiters actively use it
6. Instagram

Remember, recruiters use these services both to search for candidates and to vet them. To the latter point, 55 percent of recruiters have reconsidered a candidate after checking their feeds—and not necessarily in a positive way. According to Time.com, the majority, 61 percent of those reviews, left a negative impression. Learn from the many Googleable folks who have lost jobs for posting stupid shit online; don't give recruiters a reason to reject you before you even start.

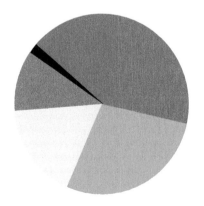

WHERE YOU SHOULD BUILD YOUR BRAND

- Linkedin
- Blog
- Twitter
- Facebook
- Everywhere Else

"Brand You" Content

Now, it's pretty clear where you'll be spending your branding time online. But what do you fill all those channels with? Recruiters and potential employers will look for three main things: a demonstrated ability to do the job at hand, some indication of what kind of employee you'll be, and your personality. While all of these things will be imperfectly represented across LinkedIn, your blog, Twitter, and wherever else you choose to share content about yourself, they will still undoubtedly create an impression. The content you share will, by and large, have the biggest impact on what that impression is.

CAN YOU DO THE JOB?

It may seem obvious to you that you can do the job you're applying for, but that may not be the case from an employer's or recruiter's perspective. To convince them that you warrant a phone or in-person interview, you'll need more than just work examples or slugs bulleting a list of accomplishments.

Every job requires specific, tangible things—such as meeting deadlines or manufacturing products—as well as intangibles, like stress management or interpersonal skills. Your goal is to show prospective employers examples of the relevant work you've done. And it really doesn't hurt if you can also show that you were able to get that work done while dealing with particular environmental factors—say, tight deadlines, stress, competing priorities, etc.

LinkedIn is probably the best tool for answering the question of whether or not you can do the job in the minds of employers and recruiters. Besides letting you share examples of your work, LinkedIn also allows you to solicit and share recommendations from current and past colleagues. This gives you the opportunity to show your work, as well as have peers contextualize it.

WHAT KIND OF EMPLOYEE ARE YOU?

Showing that you can do the required work is essential. Still, the reality of the contemporary economy is that the vast majority of jobs can be done by an ever-growing number of people. For example, last year, almost half a million people graduated from college with a business degree, according to the Pew Research Center. That's a *lot* of people who already meet the basic hiring requirements for many entry-level positions.

> "For better or worse, our company is a reflection of my thinking, my character, my values."
>
> — RUPERT MURDOCH

As important as being able to do the work at hand is how you're going to do it. Will you be a curmudgeon? A team player? Enthusiastic? Proactive? Do the bare minimum? Given the choice between two candidates that demonstrate an ability to do a job, employers will choose the one that they'll have an easier time working with. A big part of making yourself attractive to employers is showing them that you can get the work done pleasantly. An easy way to do this is to share articles and resources related to your experience and expertise.

Specificity in your posts and shares is key. You want the majority of what you share to be directly related to your job experience and responsibilities. For example, if you work in customer experience, keep your posts about market conditions or how the company should work to improve revenue to a minimum. While it's great to show some initiative, the more time you spend talking through other people's responsibilities, the less opportunity you'll have to showcase your own strengths. Employers want engaged, proactive employees. If you're demonstrating an interest both specific to and beyond your responsibilities, you'll be giving potential employers a positive impression of what kind of hire you'll be.

When it comes down to showing your interest and engagement as far as what sort of employee you'd be, LinkedIn, Twitter, and your personal blog are all good channels to use. They are appropriate places to share articles related to your work, company, or industry, as well as to open discussions, share resources, and ask for help in a big-picture way. That said, you should never share specifics about what you're working on publically. That's a pretty good way to get fired.

WHAT KIND OF PERSON ARE YOU?

To some extent, your personality will be on display throughout your online profile. That said, it's incredibly important to remember that things like tone don't always come through the way you might intend them to. If you don't want people to take something you share the wrong way, make sure it's straightforward, leaving as little room for interpretation as possible. It's paramount, when posting material online, that you focus on the intent of what you're sharing. Are you sharing something because it's funny? Then ask yourself, is it funny to just the people in your feed or to all the billion-plus people on Facebook?

The upside of digital media is that you can, to some extent, create and manage a reputation and brand for yourself—a brand that can help you get the jobs you want. The downside is that, because it's an impersonal, public medium, you're going to have to be self-aware about what you post.

Most recruiters and hiring managers note that they don't primarily look at social media other than for a reason to not hire a candidate. Still, often what they find there provides a reason. On the other hand, social media can provide a forum for sharing interests outside of work, such as volunteering and community involvement.

LinkedIn is the only place you *shouldn't* share non–work-related information. While many people do treat it like Facebook, all that does is tell recruiters and hiring managers that you don't know what the service is.

A Cautionary Tale

What you distribute through your personal brand channels will largely be shaped by the industry you work in, or want to work in, and your role within that industry. That said, perhaps the most problematic part of tailoring a personal brand in order to get hired is the potential for overshooting the mark—for being *too* enthusiastic in your approach.

The Eight Rules of Personal Branding

RULE #1: If you don't make the effort, Google will make it for you.

RULE #2: No one has total control over how others perceive them.

RULE #3: Don't assume a job requires anything more specific than the job requirements.

RULE #4: Personal branding is best practiced moderately.

RULE #5: Actively using LinkedIn is the most effective way to benefit from social media when looking for a job.

RULE #6: From the recruiter's perspective, what you see is what you get. Make sure your social media profiles don't work against you.

RULE #7: Work for clients is private; never share specifics about it publically.

RULE #8: "Imitation is the sincerest form of flattery."

For example, consider the cautionary tale of Aleksey Vayner, producer of the infamous "Impossible Is Nothing" video resume and one of the Internet's earlier victims of unintended celebrity. (Google it and watch.) In the video, Vayner presents the kind of qualities that he probably assumed the banking and investment firm UBS was looking for: confidence, assuredness, insightfulness, intelligence, passion, and all the other qualities of Wall Street alpha males. Unfortunately for Vayner, UBS was more likely looking for someone who would just keep their mouth shut in front of clients, take direction, and not do anything stupid. While the video is comedic throughout, it is, essentially, a person trying *way too hard* to brand himself in order to influence a hiring decision. Needless to say, he didn't get the job.

Beyond the Big Three

Besides the major qualities future employers look for in your online presence—job skills, what kind of employee you are, and what your personality is—there are a handful of other ways to round out your personal brand for the better.

BIG-PICTURE CONTENT

Do some research on leaders in your field of work. Identify those people and follow at least five of them on social media. In all likelihood, they will be posting, tweeting, and sharing insights and commentary on the trends you need to be aware of. They'll share what sources they read and who they think are doing progressive and cutting-edge work and provide industry forecasts. If you find yourself agreeing with someone most of the time, bingo, you've got a role model to follow. Just as important, however, is to find people who disagree with your role models or offer a counterpoint to the prevailing wisdom.

DRILL DOWN

Once you've identified some professional guides that are helping you understand the big picture, get specific about your role within that industry. In all likelihood, somewhere in the vastness of the Internet exists discussion groups, Reddits, meetups, and any number of other resources discussing, specifically, what the day-to-day issues of your ideal job are. The more specific you can get, the more credibility you'll create in the minds of recruiters and potential employers.

DON'T BE AFRAID TO NAME-DROP

Big names carry an institutional caché that can work in your favor. Being a project manager at General Electric is a completely different read than a being a project manager at Dave and Sons transmission manufacturing. If you've had a role in a big flashy project or done work for some important clients, don't be afraid to brag a little bit. "Dave, who worked for Apple" is a lot more memorable for recruiters and hiring managers than is just "Dave."

TIE IT ALL TOGETHER

Employers aren't really looking for people who share a ton of scattered information, job experience, and skills. You need to be able to wrestle that information into a cohesive narrative—one that informs your particular take on the responsibilities of your role in a company. Once you do that, you'll have created a distinctive brand in the minds of potential employers.

Offline Branding

Despite the seeming omnipresence of the Internet, you still have to meet someone in real life in order to land a job. For that reason, it's hugely important that you take as much care grooming your physical presence as your online one. Beyond appearance and hygiene, it's important to understand what qualities employers value in candidates and, to the extent possible, embody them—or at least work examples of them into face-to-face meetings. If you've made it to in-person interviews, then you can be reasonably assured that the recruiter and hiring manager feel you've got the skills and experience necessary for the position. At this point of the hiring process, you're being vetted as to whether or not you'd be a good "fit" for the team you'd be working with.

Every organization has its own culture—a product of the historical successes, failures, and leadership of that company—and will value candidates according to how well their personalities fit that culture. Some businesses give preference to thoughtfulness over decisiveness; others value ambition over teamwork. Before you head into your interviews, it's a good idea to know what those values are. Once you do, speak to how they inform your work ethic.

Of course, not all desirable professional qualities are industry specific. There are a number of cross-industry qualities that almost all employers look for. The following are baseline characteristics you want people to associate with your personality.

ENTHUSIASM

Not everyone gets to be passionate about what they do. Even so, you do have to present an interest beyond, "I'm just here for the money." If all other considerations are equal, an employer will hire a candidate who appears more interested and engaged with the work at hand than one who is competent but couldn't care less. You can express enthusiasm by talking about big-picture trends affecting the company, by asking about and spitballing solutions for problems the position will be responsible for addressing, or by showing some interest in the industry beyond what is required of the job you're applying for.

ACCOUNTABILITY

Most people think of accountability as a reactive quality: "That was my fault." But it's not just about owning up to your mistakes. Just as you might be responsible for a problem, you are also responsible for coming up with solutions. Recognizing all the things that you're responsible for demonstrates to employers your initiative and independence. During your interview, it's very likely that you're going to be asked to walk your interviewers through a project that you succeeded or failed at. This is a perfect moment to work in your awareness of what being an accountable employee is.

FLEXIBILITY

It's the nature of business to seek efficiency. That means that if your boss can get away with you filling in on a project outside of your direct responsibility, he or she will probably at least try to. Being flexible is an essential part of teamwork, and it's a really good idea to come to an interview with an example or nine of how you have graciously demonstrated flexibility, at prior jobs or otherwise. Discussing flexibility is an ideal way to showcase a skill or experience that may not be directly related to the job at hand, but can open up the interviewer's understanding of your capabilities.

INTERPERSONAL SKILLS

Possibly the only job left in the world that doesn't require a basic understanding of how to politely and respectfully interact with people is the customer service desk at the DMV or any major metropolitan impound lot. You don't have to be able to sell dirt to farmers, but you do need some baseline of people skills. Recognize if someone is uncomfortable and how to make them feel better; know how to stay focused on what's being discussed; make a mental note of follow-up questions; and practice for when there are lulls in conversation. Your friends and family may think you're cracking up, but talking through scenarios out loud is not a bad idea.

MENTORSHIP

One of the most underrated qualities an employee can bring to an organization is the ability and willingness to help other people get better at their job. You literally help yourself by helping the company when you make the time to assist colleagues with things they don't know how to do. It will come back to you, like a great big hug in the form of salary-increase potential, when your coworkers fill out performance reports. So, be prepared to show a prospective employer how you helped less-experienced employees learn the ropes or how you took it upon yourself to learn a new platform or software that you then shared with other employees.

Building your brand is largely a balancing act between self-awareness and authenticity. You want to share your accomplishments and highlight your strengths, both as you perceive them and in the words of peers, former employers, and coworkers. In the next chapter, we'll look less at tooting your own horn and more at what you can do to be a good online citizen.

GET IT DONE

1. Choose five professional, industry role models to learn from. Follow their social media accounts and read up on any books, articles, or presentations they've given. X *Time on task: 1–2 hrs, books notwithstanding.*

2. Solidify your brand by (1) identifying the strengths you can bring to an employer, (2) highlighting the skills your target job requires, and (3) finding the opportunity where required skills and your strengths cross over. X *Time on task: 0–1 hrs.*

3. Start telling your story through your online channels. X *Time on task: 15–30 mins, daily.*

Resources

Ries. Al and Jack Trout. *Positioning: The Battle for Your Mind.* **New York: McGraw-Hill, 2001.**
A must-read book for anyone interested in understanding why people choose one thing over another and the tools advertisers use to influence those choices.

AllTop.com
AllTop lets you search blogs via subjects they're publishing. It's a great way to find existing experts as well as audiences that may be receptive to your own point of view.

"Me, Inc.," Ann Friedman. *The New Republic,* **September 28, 2015.**
www.newrepublic.com/article/122910/my-paradoxical-quest
-build-personal-brand
Taking to heart that Intuit is predicting 40 percent of the United States workforce will be freelance by 2020, the author sets off on a quest to make sure she's ready for a self-reliant future. It's a good read on the successes and failures of setting up your own brand.

MarketingProfs.com: Search > personal branding
This is a great all-around resource for marketing, branding, personal branding, and a host of other subjects that will come in handy during your job search. While the site requires registration, it's free and worth giving up your email for access.

bVcard.com
This service lets you create a virtual business card (.vcf file) that you can send via email and post on your website, blog, or LinkedIn. It will also show up in search results.

CHAPTER SIX

BE A DIGITAL NATIVE

READING TIME ⏳ 30–40 MINUTES

What Is a Digital Native?

The term *digital native* was coined in 2001 by Marc Prensky, CEO of Games2Train, an education company that bases its pedagogy in the digital gaming environment. Prensky splits society into two camps: those who were born after 1980, digital natives, and those born before, digital immigrants.

Prensky's focus wasn't so much on the hardware and ubiquity of computing and the Internet as it was on the cultural changes those technologies created. Kids born after 1980 grew up in a world in which art, politics, economics, religious practices, and other expressions of culture were affected and changed by computers and the Internet. His central point is that educators need to take those changes into account when thinking about how to best teach students in the information age.

The news media grazed over Prensky's focus on education and turned his observations into a "versus" story: old people can't compete with young people in a job marketplace dominated by familiarity with digital technology. The stories kicked around long enough to change the public's perception of what the term *digital native* meant. As recently as 2012, this same storyline enjoyed a second wind as the last of the paper-based news organizations moved into online business models. Digital marketing agencies, responding to massive budget shifts favoring online advertising, began seeking digital natives for specific roles, thinking they could better communicate with the coveted 18 to 34 demographic. *Digital immigrants* became synonymous with an inauthentic understanding of the Internet. Again, the news media were quick to produce stories of generational warfare; fear of obsolescence is a great way to grab the attention of digital immigrants.

As with most technologies that purportedly disrupt society, the truth of the matter is where digital natives and digital immigrants meet. Computers and the Internet have fundamentally changed almost every aspect of society. But, those changes have affected both sides of Prensky's divide. The "Greatest Generation" and Baby Boomers forced subsequent generations to adapt to their customs just as much as they have been forced to adapt to Gen X, Gen Y, and the Millennials. Meaning, what is considered acceptable conduct online is the product of a multi-generational conversation that's been taking place for decades both online and off.

Whatever Prensky's original intention, being a digital native in contemporary culture has as much to do with your online etiquette as it does with the digital tools themselves. It's important to understand how the formal expectations of business culture and the informal, autonomous nature of the Internet interact.

Always On

Here's a riddle: What follows you everywhere, incessantly demands your attention, derails your train of thought, interrupts your conversations, and never apologizes? You and more than three billion other people in the world know the answer: the Internet. Here are a few truths about life online.

TRUTH #1: CONVENIENCE CREATES EXPECTATIONS ABOUT TIMELINESS

How many times has someone sent you a text, followed shortly by an impatient second, "Hello?" Digital communications create expectations in their users that can mirror the qualities of the medium they are using. In this case, because it's so convenient to send someone a message, there's an assumption that it's equally convenient to respond. It's an intrusive trade-off for the convenience the Internet provides. Such convenience has been codified in many industries. In tech, financial services, retail, and other areas of employment, companies have instituted rules regarding the amount of time that passes between receiving a communication and responding to it; if you take too long, sometimes only 12 hours, it can be grounds for getting fired.

TRUTH #2: ADAPTIVE TECHNOLOGIES NECESSITATE FLEXIBLE USERS

As anyone who has ever experienced an email chain spiraling off topic can attest to, the Internet is by no means static. Its malleability has had far-reaching consequences, both socially and in the business world.

Here's a quick, and probably familiar, social example: Do you have any friends who wait until the last minute to commit to a plan? It may be partly who they are, but it's also partly the ease of communication that makes it unnecessary to make a plan ahead of time. You can just wing it or wait for better options.

In business there's a phenomenon called the Agile school of management. Agile management came out of the failure of assembly-line production as a model for software programming. For decades, the dominant model of production in business wasn't much different than Henry Ford's factory lines. You build the product, one step at a time. It works fine for physical products, but not so well for digital ones. Not only does the digital environment change too quickly, but it's also more efficient to build software in tandem to troubleshoot bugs, adapt to new needs, and adjust to changing business goals.

TRUTH #3: PUBLIC SHARING AND PUBLIC SHAMING ARE TWO ENDS OF THE SAME STREET

The Internet, and its accessible broadcast platforms, is anything but intimate—but many people forget this. Whatever you put on social media is accessible to almost every other person on social media. This fact has gotten a lot of people in trouble. Here are just a few examples.

▶ (Former) Congressman Anthony Weiner resigned after he sent pictures of his penis to women he met over social media.

▶ Wisconsin State Congressman Dane Deutsch lost his election bid after tweeting that Abraham Lincoln and Adolph Hitler were both strong leaders.

▶ Radio host Anthony Cumia of "Anthony & Opie" was fired after sharing racist tweets.

▶ PR heavyweight Justine Sacco likely tanked her career forever in 2013 when she tweeted, "Going to Africa. Hope I don't get AIDS. Just kidding, I'm white."

It's important to keep these truths in mind—particularly if you want to stay hirable in the eyes of employers.

Good Online Citizenship

Before you start polishing your online profile, do what any prospective employer or recruiter will do first: Google yourself. Go ahead. I'll wait.

What comes up? Do the search results paint a picture that says, "Yeah, this guy looks like someone we should bring in for an interview?" Or does it come back neutral or negative? It's important that search results around your name be overwhelmingly positive for two reasons. The first is that nearly all recruiters, headhunters, and hiring managers will do this right off the bat when considering candidates. The second reason, according to Kelly Milner, a recruiter specializing in locating design talent, is that recruiters spend five or six seconds looking at a candidate's profile before deciding to call someone in or not. Remember the rule of thumb regarding your online presence and getting hired: don't give them a reason not to hire you.

The Seven Rules of Online Citizenship

RULE #1: Do unto others. If you're posting about someone else, make sure you'd be ok with them posting the same thing about you. Would it sting if someone said it about you? Would you be okay with the picture if it was your face?

RULE #2: Obey the law. Is what you are doing violating the law? If you have to ask that question, whatever it is you're about to "share" shouldn't make it out of the room.

RULE #3: Don't follow the crowd. Just because everyone else is doing it, it is not a good reason for you to be doing it, too. Crowds have terrible moral compasses—and even worse decision-making abilities. If everyone else is doing it, you probably shouldn't be.

RULE #4: Be clear. If you're not sure how something you share will be perceived, you should probably not share it. It's best to be obvious to the point of transparent than to try and explain yourself in 40-character exchanges.

RULE #5: Be yourself. Don't think you can maintain an online personality that is separate from your offline one—there's no separation. If you're uncomfortable with the idea of posting something, remember, it informs who you are no matter where you are.

RULE #6: Take a deep breath. The Internet attracts wrath like a mosquito attracts slapping hands. If you're angry with someone, take a breath, walk around the block, talk to a friend, watch a movie, go to bed, wake up, take a bike ride, and then consider responding to them—just not online.

RULE #7: No assumptions. Don't think that you can tell how someone might react to a post or comment, no matter how well you know them.

If you ever come across someone breaking these rules, call them out on it. You may not change their behavior, but you can set a good example by trying.

How to Change Google Results

Quite a few variables can affect what Google returns—and what a potential employer might see in their first, critical assessment of you. The way Google works (and this is to grossly oversimplify billions of dollars of math and computing) is to find all the things associated with your name, weigh the connections between them and the kind of site hosting the content your name appears in, and make a list. That said, there are two main ways you can affect your Google results: post lots and link lots.

METHOD #1: POST LOTS OF CONTENT

Again, to greatly simplify, you can affect your search results by creating a lot of content about yourself. While things do get more difficult if a lot of people share your name, the process is essentially the same: Post more stuff.

If you're like most people, your Google search results probably returned some social network links and some generic information from aggregator sites such as Spokeo, Intelius, and RealDirect. These aggregator sites pull their information from social media sites, as well as phone books and government databases like those containing real estate transactions. The good news is that you can affect these third-party results by sharing lots of content on the sites you do control.

METHOD 2: LINK YOUR CONTENT THROUGHOUT YOUR ONLINE PROFILE CHANNELS

The other way you can influence what comes up in your search results is by linking all of the content you're creating. Google weighs a site linked to another site more favorably than it does stand-alone sites. So, if you have a blog or personal website, make sure that your website links to your blog, social media profiles, and any other channels you may have. Do the same, to the extent allowed by the services you are using, with all of your online profile components. If diagramed, you want your online profile to look like this, with each of the outer nodes being each of your online channels:

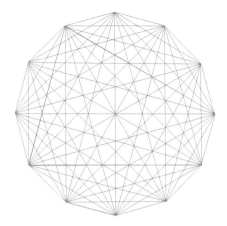

And that's about all you can do, for free, to make sure the results page of a Google search for your name returns content you've created. You can request that Google take down sensitive information such as your signature, Social Security number, compromising pictures, etc., but your best bet is to not share that kind of content with anyone to begin with.

> "Where do you hide a dead body? On the third page of Google results."
>
> —LORI RANDALL STRADTMAN

What to Scrub

Just as creating content for potential employers to find is important, so is scrubbing the content you are already broadcasting to the world. We already covered the main no-no's of posting online earlier, so I'll just briefly summarize them again here. Don't post any of this:

- ▶ Racism, sexism, misogyny, homophobia
- ▶ Endorsement of violence
- ▶ Conspiracy theories about what the Egyptian pyramids were "actually" used for

- ▶ Excessive or irresponsible use of alcohol
- ▶ Anything illegal
- ▶ Nudity and pornography

Additionally, you'll want to make sure that your online profiles are free of bad grammar, are factually correct, and are consistent across your channels. Nobody likes to hire a dummy or a liar.

Shit Happened. What Can You Do?

Your ability to change search results or scrub undesirable content about yourself is almost entirely dependent on whether or not you "own" the channel the content is on—in other words, did you create the profile or not. If you didn't set up the account, you're largely at the mercy of the owner.

What Can I Change?

CAN CHANGE EASILY	CAN'T CHANGE EASILY (OR AT ALL)
Your Blog	News sites
LinkedIn	Other people's blogs
Twitter	Other people's websites
Facebook	Other people's social media accounts
Google+	
Instagram	
All other social channels you set up	

Going Mobile

The boom in smart phone usage is reorienting society around its preferred uses, habits, and features. The business of recruiting candidates and finding jobs is no exception. According to a recent Talent HQ survey, Americans are performing more than a billion job searches on their mobile phones every month. HR departments are responding to this by building out applications and search processes that are easier to execute on your phone.

The big reason behind the push for going mobile is that recruiters are, more or less, guaranteed to reach the candidates they are searching for, in part due to demographic shifts. Younger people tend to favor mobile platforms more than desktops, and more of the workforce than ever is using mobile technology. Mobile recruiting uses all of the same techniques and tools that desktop-based recruiting does—job boards, social media, and software programs that do keyword searches. Recruiters and prospective employers have to go where the searches are happening.

Mobile recruiting really breaks down some of the formalities normally associated with the job search. Recruiters and candidates routinely text one another as part of the process. Interviews often happen over FaceTime, wherever the candidate happens to be, as long as it's not too noisy. This lack of formality is probably just a recognition that mobile recruiting can be invasive and if, as a headhunter, you're going to engage in it, you'll have to deal with people as they are in their everyday lives.

To take advantage of mobile recruiting as a job seeker, you'll need all of your work-related info available in a mobile-friendly format, such as a vCard (.vcf file) or a PDF saved on your smartphone. When a recruiter contacts you or when you're filling out an online application, you can share your vCard instead of typing in the info—saving you time and preventing you from having to fat-finger your way through a series of tiny boxes on a multiple-page application. vCards are great because you can include basic contact info, such as your mobile number and email, as well as links to your LinkedIn profile, Twitter handle, Facebook profile, and personal website and blog. Better yet, create a link to a one-stop site of everything recruiters and potential employers need to see.

Mobile recruiting is mostly focused on entry-level, temporary, retail, and unskilled labor positions—a boon for recent college grads. If you're looking for your first job or a gap to make ends meet while you plot out your takeover of the legal entertainment industry, a mobile-centric search could be ideal for your needs.

The Five URLs That Will Define Your Career

There are a huge number of services, platforms, and channels available to you online. But, as far as job-hunting goes, only five of them play a significant role in a potential employer hiring you:

1. **Your Google search results.** If it seems like I keep harping on about this, that's only because it's that big of a deal. Depending on what comes up, you'll be "in consideration" or forgotten before a recruiter types another name into the search bar.

2. **A personal website or blog.** All of the recruiters and hiring managers I talked to for this book said that they'd click on a personal website or blog before they would check out your LinkedIn profile. So, if you have the time, resources, and energy to make one, do it.

3. **LinkedIn.** If you have a website or blog, LinkedIn is probably going to fall under the "due diligence" column as far as recruiters and hiring managers are concerned. If you don't, then this is one spot they'll be sure to check for engagement, professionalism, work history, and examples.

4. **Twitter.** If a recruiter or hiring manager is taking the time to look at your Twitter feed, you should be ecstatic. Make sure there's some interesting stuff on there, though.

5. **Facebook.** Depending on the circumstances surrounding the job opportunity, a recruiter may go to Facebook before Instagram or your other profiles. Why? To see if they can find anything to rule you out and winnow down the pool of applicants. But it's more likely for a potential employer to surf your non–work-related social accounts as cleanup.

We'll get into the particulars of how to optimize each channel in later chapters. For now, just know where each of them stands in the mind of a recruiter looking to fill job vacancies and trim the fat from their already bloated list of potential hires.

In this chapter, we've covered what it takes to be a respectable online citizen, as well as how to go about polishing your search results. In the next few chapters, we'll take a detailed look at how to optimize each of your online profiles.

GET IT DONE

1. Google yourself. Make note of what you find, particularly if anything problematic hits the first or second page of results. ⧗ *Time on task: 20 mins.*

2. Jump straight into scrubbing your online profile of any profanity, racism, drug use, bad grammar, and whatever other no-no's on our list you may have posted online. ⧗ *Time on task: 20–40 mins.*

3. Prep your mobile search tools. Pull together a vCard or QR code to a one-stop you shop, where recruiters can access all of your online profiles. ⧗ *Time on task: 1 hr.*

Resources

Naymz

www.naymz.com/

The pay for social reputation management businesses is growing like gangbusters. Namyz, along with BrandYourself and many others, is one of many services in the area. There are some very basic features you can use by providing an email but, for the most part, it's a pay-to-play business.

Google Alerts

www.google.com/alerts

Through this service, you can get notified anytime someone posts something that includes your name. Through the "settings" option, you can select sources, frequency of reports, and other options. It's a passive way to keep track of what you, or your doppelgängers, are up to online.

Carr, Nicholas. *The Shallows: What the Internet Is Doing to Our Brains.* **New York: W.W. Norton & Company, 2011.**
Just as the Internet and its associated technologies have transformed culture, there's growing evidence that it is also affecting human biology and psychology. Carr's bestseller delves into those changes with unsettling depth.

Ted Talks, Jon Ronson:
When Online Shaming Spirals out of Control
http://www.ted.com/talks/jon_ronson_what_happens_when_online_shaming_spirals_out_of_control
The author of *So You've been Publically Shamed* gives an engaging overview of what happens to people when the Internet, or more pointedly, its users, turn against them. He covers several prominent examples, including Jonah Lehrer and Justine Sacco, but the real kicker is how quickly the court of public opinion can spiral out of control.

How People Are Changing Their Own Behavior
www.pewinternet.org/2015/03/16/how-people-are-changing-their-own-behavior/
This Pew Research Center report quantifies some of the terrifying ways that Internet users are self-censoring and modifying their behavior online due to government surveillance and public shaming.

CHAPTER SEVEN

LINKEDIN: THE BIG TENT

READING TIME 30–40 MINUTES

Who Uses LinkedIn?

Before we get into the details of how LinkedIn's business environment can help you land a job, it's helpful to know who's on it and why they use it. Here are some stats from ExpandedRamblings.com to give you a big-picture idea of who makes up LinkedIn's more than 400 million global user base:

- ► One in three professionals on the planet are on LinkedIn.
- ► 41 percent of the world's millionaires use the service.
- ► 44 percent of LinkedIn members are female, 56 percent are male.
- ► About 75 percent of users are between the ages of 25 and 54.
- ► Education, information technology, financial services, and retail are the most represented industries.
- ► LinkedIn represents workers from more than 200 countries.

While these stats can give you a general idea of who's on the platform, keep in mind that things change quickly. In 2013, LinkedIn had about 150 million users and, as of writing, was adding two new users every second. Some of the company's strongest growth is in

Asia; Indonesia, for example, has more LinkedIn users than Facebook users. CEO Jeff Weiner is projecting that the service's user base will top out at just over three billion, making it three times the size of Facebook. (But take that three billion-plus number with a grain of salt: That's every employee on the planet.)

Everything in Its Right Place

More important than who uses LinkedIn is what they use it for. This may seem obvious at first glance, but the biggest differentiator, which has been a huge factor in its success, for LinkedIn's intent is to be a business-oriented platform. It's an essential difference for job seekers to understand because it completely shifts the goalposts on what is, or isn't, appropriate and, more important, expected by people using the service. LinkedIn users are, on the whole, focused on business-related activities, including:

▶ Researching businesses and companies

▶ Networking with existing business contacts

▶ Building relationships with influencers

▶ Building relationships with customers

▶ Job prospecting

▶ Marketing

▶ Sales prep

▶ Sales

On LinkedIn, anything related to business is fair game. When you're on LinkedIn, you must come to terms with and accept the fact that people will be asking you for job advice, for help searching, if you know of anyone hiring, how you solved a particular work issue, and any number of business-related possibilities. People expect to be hit up for jobs, connections, introductions, and anything else that falls under the rubric of business. Of course, there are rules, especially when you're trying to get help from people you don't actually know.

Strengths for Job Seekers

LinkedIn has built a number of different features that can help you in your job search.

CONNECTIONS

LinkedIn's most basic function is to build a personal network out of your contacts. This can come from any number of different places, including your email database, Facebook network, or other social media accounts. Connections can help your cause in a couple of ways. They make it very easy to broadcast that you're looking for a job and to personally contact individuals you might think can help. Additionally, while your own network might not be able to help, someone in it may have someone in their own network who can.

JOB SEARCH

Searching for a new position through LinkedIn is pretty cool. Depending on your needs, you can filter by geographic location, industry, salary, keywords, and a few other options. What's more, when you find a job you feel might be a good fit, there's often a hiring manager you can contact directly attached to it. The importance of this function really cannot be overstated. Besides, if you're relying solely on job boards, you're depending on a software program kicking your resume up to the hiring manager. Job search lets you be a bit more proactive. Also, as Ryan Woodring noted, "I won't consider someone who doesn't reach out. I'm only going to hire people who are interested enough to find the job, not the other way around."

PASSIVE CANDIDACY

Passive candidates are people who aren't actively looking for work but are open to receiving offers or discussing opportunities. While that might seem like everyone, the important distinction is that passive candidacy is made possible by online technology and services. If you're on LinkedIn, it means that you're open to fielding calls from recruiters. If you join LinkedIn or any other service that shares your work history publically or semi-publically, recruiters and hiring managers consider you fair game.

"That's one of the biggest uses of the service," notes Kelly Milner. "I've had people say 'No thanks, but let's keep in touch,' but no one has ever gotten upset that I contacted them about an open position. Most people understand it's all about networking. Just because someone isn't open to considering a new role right now doesn't mean they won't be in a few months or even a year or two down the road. I like to build long-term relationships, not just thinking about what is available now but what might come in the future."

GROUPS

LinkedIn does not restrict with whom you can connect. It's one of the firewall features built into the service that helps cut down on spam and reinforces the prime goal of the site: creating networks of people who are already connected. You can, however, get introduced to people you are not directly connected with through people you are directly connected to. The Group function is another way to expand your network and meet other users. Groups are usually centered on a particular industry or skill set, and anyone can start one. For example, you could join the iOS Developers group where you'll meet 79,518 other people interested, and presumably working in, the iOS environment. Once your application to the group has been accepted—as easy as clicking on a "join" button—you will be able to message the whole group or individuals and ask to connect to them.

Weaknesses for Job Seekers

Some of LinkedIn's weaknesses are self-made, and some are the unfortunate by-product of the exponential growth available to online services. Here's where LinkedIn doesn't do such a great job.

SITE-WIDE AUTOMATIC MODERATION (SWAM)

As LinkedIn grew from big to gigantic, the task of making sure the service's Groups feature didn't get flooded with spam became an increasingly difficult one to solve without automation. Moderators and administrators can only keep track of so many communications in the groups they've set up, and with some groups reaching

730,000-plus members, it's impossible to physically monitor what's a legitimate contribution and what isn't. In a nutshell, if a group moderator removes you from their group or deletes or blocks a comment, you get removed from all the groups you're a member of. While this is more of a technical glitch than anything, and LinkedIn is working to fix the issue, it's a downside, for sure.

SCALE

As LinkedIn grows bigger, it is becoming more attractive to the marketing and advertising industries in good and bad ways. According to AdAge.com, advertising constitutes about 30 percent of the site's revenue and is obviously important for its continued existence. But, under the cover of sharing content, marketers and advertisers are flooding user feeds with unhelpful or useless information. This is a unscientific example, but I counted about an equal number of personal posts in my feed vs. posts selling things. "Check out the 'white label' direct mail platform used by the BIGGEST brands in the world. Does your agency or franchise need a better way to sell and manage direct mail services?" In part, this is because LinkedIn's feed features its lucrative "native advertising" product; those posts that look like news stories but are in fact advertisements. So the service's feed is a hodgepodge of your connections' stories and insight, and a lot of marketing pitches.

CONNECTIONS

Although considered a strength for the service, connections cut both ways. LinkedIn was designed around the idea that the personal network is an individual's strongest asset in business. But, at the end of the day, the platform provides a virtual network, not a physical one. For job seekers, the best possible thing to do in order to enjoy a long, thriving career is develop as many personal, real-world connections as they can. LinkedIn is an elegant support system for real-world networks, but it will never replace actually working with people, developing relationships, and going through the fire together.

LinkedIn Profile Checklist

SUMMARY	The summary is basically a cover letter about yourself. It's a space where you get to give an overview of your career and what you love about your vocation.
EXPERIENCE	The site will ask you to fill in discrete sections related to different jobs you've had. You can take the standard route and bullet point a bunch of stuff, but you're probably better off writing a descriptive paragraph that encapsulates your accomplishments in each position. Don't make it a resume; think back to your personal brand in chapter 5 and tell a story.
BACKGROUND IMAGE	Your profile allows for a 1400 × 425 pixel banner you can upload an image to. Make sure it's representative of your work strengths.
PORTRAIT	You get a maximum 500 × 500 pixel photo to accompany your summary. Again, make sure it's business appropriate.
WORK EXAMPLES	Think of this as you might a professional portfolio. You can upload several examples of work you've done alongside the corresponding job in your experience section. PDF or .jpeg files are the most compatible.
LINKS TO PERSONAL WEBSITES AND BLOGS	You don't need to do much with this; just cut and paste in the URLs.
EDUCATION	Here you can list your academic achievements, degrees, GPAs, and even include pictures of your diploma(s) if the spirit moves you.
CERTIFICATIONS	As with education, here you can link to any certificates you care to share.
ADDITIONAL INFO	In case their template missed anything, LinkedIn gives you a space to share more information. Most people use this section for hobbies and interests.

Ace Your Profile

Now that we've looked at LinkedIn's ups and downs, let's get to the meat of this section: how to tweak your profile to help you get a job, new job, or dream job. The advice that follows is both a procedural take on how to get it done right, as well as learned examples of members doing their best to look unattractive.

Before you start, you'll need some work-related materials on hand; it's way easier to get this stuff done ahead of time and cut and paste it into your profile than it is to type it out as you go.

Once you have all the elements together, start optimizing your profile. The following tips are based around best practices related to searches, keywords, and other rules of LinkedIn as a platform.

PRO TIP #1: CUSTOMIZE YOUR PROFILE URL

While it may seem more aesthetic than anything else, customizing your profile URL does help with the overall professional presentation you want to stick to. In the upper right-hand corner of your profile template, you'll see something that looks like this:

Your public profile URL

Enhance your personal brand by creating a custom URL for your LinkedIn public profile.

www.linkedin.com/in/jdillahunt

Change it to your name, personal website, or whatever you'd like. Whatever you decide, it'll be better than the gobbledygook LinkedIn spits out as your URL when you create your account.

PRO TIP #2: PACK YOUR SUMMARY WITH KEYWORDS

LinkedIn gives preference to certain areas of your profile over others when figuring out how to weigh search results. An unobtrusive way to do this is to end your summary with keywords that describe your background, something like: "Skills: F16 pilot, barehanded wood-chopper, writer of poems, saver of puppies . . . " Be sure to add five or so keyword terms related to your work experience.

PRO TIP #3: GET 500-PLUS CONNECTIONS

Aim to have a minimum of 500 connections; the *plus* is essentially infinite. While the downside of having more connections is a cluttered feed, this is far outweighed by the upside. LinkedIn weighs search results in part by the degree of the connection. That is to say, if someone is directly connected to you, you'll show up higher in their search results than someone who is a second-tier connection and friend of a friend as it were. So, if a recruiter or hiring manager is looking to fill a position, you'll have a better chance of popping up high in their search results by being directly connected with them.

PRO TIP #4: ADD A PICTURE

While adding a photo to your profile may seem like an aesthetic no-brainer (nobody likes to connect to a faceless profile), there's actual data behind it: profiles without a picture get passed over 60 percent more often than those that have a picture.

PRO TIP #5: BE SELECTIVE IN YOUR ENDORSEMENTS

It's better to have more endorsements in fewer categories than fewer endorsements in more categories. We live in an age of specialization; packing all of your endorsements into a few categories will reinforce that.

PRO TIP #6: CHANGE YOUR WEBSITE'S ANCHOR TEXT TO SOMETHING READABLE

You can link personal websites and blogs to your LinkedIn profile. Normally, the link would look something like www.yourwebsite.com /wordpress/yourname, but you can change the display to whatever you'd like through the website tab in your profile.

PRO TIP #7: YOU CAN REARRANGE THE TEMPLATE ORDER OF YOUR PROFILE

Summary	↕

In the upper right-hand corner of each section of your profile, you'll find up and down arrows. Use these to move sections around to hit people viewing your profile with whatever section makes the most impact.

PRO TIP #8: GO PRIVATE WHEN MAKING CHANGES

When you make changes to your profile, you have the option of making those changes public (and every connection you have will be notified when you make them) or private. Notifying everyone every time you tweak a job profile is annoying. However, getting a new job, publishing an article, sharing a certification, or any other major change is worth sharing. Go private for the housekeeping, but keep the humble brags public.

PRO TIP #9: CHECK THE "WE HEARD YOU" PAGE

Keep in mind that LinkedIn is constantly updating and tweaking its features and services. It's a good idea to stay on top of them lest the ground has moved beneath your feet while you weren't paying attention.

Platform Etiquette

Once your profile is tight as a drum, it's time to start using the service for its intended purpose: networking. The most straightforward way to do this is to winnow down your contacts into a subset that work in the industry you're targeting. Then, further trim them into the people who do the job you want or work with those who do. After that, it's as simple as sending polite, professional notes explaining your interests and professional goals. The following are a few ways you can get connected to people outside your network—a boon for when you find the person who could be your boss someday or holds the keys to your dream job:

1. **Get introduced.** If you have a connection in common, you can ask that common acquaintance to make an introduction.

2. **Join a group.** Groups are probably the best way to get connected to someone who is completely outside of your network. In a group, you can respond to the person's posts or comments as well as share your own point of view on similar subjects. Once you've established a rapport, reach out for a connection.

3. **Cold-call them.** You can use the in-platform messaging program to contact an unconnected user, but LinkedIn limits the number of times you can do this on a monthly basis.

Always remember, however, that while LinkedIn is considered a social network, none of the casual social graces of other networks apply. When contacting anyone on the platform, even close friends, it's best to keep things professional—not formal, but professional.

What's an Appropriate Tone on LinkedIn?

NO	NO	YES
"Dude! I want a new job . . . "	"Dear Sir, I'm trying to advance . . . "	"Mr. Jones, I've been a freelance designer . . . "

While tone is hugely important, it's not the only consideration for professional networking online. Here are a few other tips.

▶ **Don't badger.** When you're asking people for help, the last thing you want to do is come across as a pest, impatient, or ungracious. If you know people personally and they don't get back to you after a first contact, you can try following up with them a few days later. If they don't follow up with you on the second contact, you might want to drop it. If you don't know them personally, you get one shot. If they want to respond to you, they will; don't convince yourself they just forgot.

▶ **Keep it short and sweet.** Clarity and brevity are also important. You've got to assume that everyone is busy, and beating around the bush won't help your cause. At the same time, you don't want to be brusque; just keep it to four or five lines. Pretty much all job-search communications will take place on the service's messaging platform that, by design, is pretty ungainly; short and sweet is your friend.

▶ **Stay active.** "If I look at a candidate's profile and it hasn't been active for a year, I'll make a note of it," says Sarah El Batanouny, a recruiter at Solomon Page that specializes in filling freelance, project, and temporary positions. She notes that it's not necessarily a negative, but when all things are equal between job candidates, the person who seems more engaged will likely prevail. This is not to say that you should treat your LinkedIn feed and group participation like you would a Twitter account. Focus and quality are more important than volume of posts. You want whatever it is you share to be directly related to the job you're seeking, or at least related to your industry. One handy way to keep your feed interesting is to summarize in a sentence or two the takeaway of what you're sharing.

Tips for Getting Hired

You can use a couple features unique to LinkedIn to help make contact with potential employers. While some of them are passive, others require some virtual elbow grease on your part. Here they are.

WHO'S VIEWED YOUR PROFILE

When you log into your account, you'll see your profile picture header at the top of the page and your feed following directly under it. To the right of that, you'll see this box:

> 5 people viewed your profile in the past 15 days
>
> ▾16% profile rank in the past 30 days

When you click on the top portion, you'll be taken to a page that shows you who found your profile via searching or reading your posts:

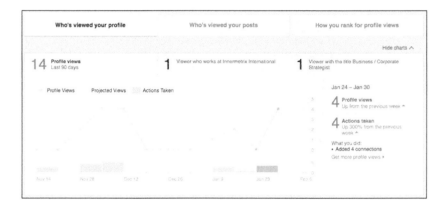

Sometimes, these views show connections who are just browsing; other times, they are recruiters and hiring managers doing research on candidates. And this is where LinkedIn's free account reaches the end of its utility. If you want to see who the people are and contact them, you'll need to upgrade to a premium, paid account. While you really don't need the paid version for 80 percent of what you're doing on LinkedIn, for job seekers, it can be pretty helpful in opening up options to contact other users.

The bottom half of the profile views section is a good indicator of how active you've been in the past month. Generally speaking, the more active and engaged you are, the higher your profile will rank.

USE THE JOBS SECTION

LinkedIn's navigation bar has a section called Jobs. Click it. It will take you to the Jobs page where you can click the "Advanced search" option to bring up something like this:

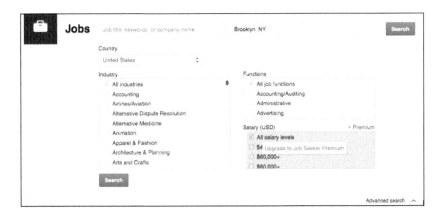

Here is where LinkedIn really proves its worth as a great service for job-hunters. In a few clicks, you can get localized results specific to your strengths. What's better, you get to see who has posted the job and, in many cases, contact them directly. It's a super-efficient way to circumvent the software programs recruiters and hiring managers use to sort through, and discard the majority of, resumes and applicants.

HIGHLIGHT VOLUNTEER WORK

While it might seem like a low priority for job seekers, highlighting volunteer work is one of many small opportunities you can take advantage of to further your job search. "I always look to see if someone has volunteer experience," says Ryan Woodring. "If I see that someone is taking the time to support a reading or arts program, I'm going to think, 'That's a nice person.' And I want to hire nice people."

We've covered a lot of ground in this chapter, but nobody said giving the bird to a vestige of old-timey employment seeking would be easy. In the next chapter, we'll look at ways you can use Facebook to your job-seeking advantage.

GET IT DONE

1. Set up your LinkedIn account. Fill out your work summary and experience. Add some work examples, a professional profile photo, and an eye-catching background image. Round everything out with links to personal websites and blogs, your education summary, certifications, and whatever volunteer experience you might have. *Time on task: 2–4 hrs.*

2. Optimize your profile. Customize your profile URL. Pack your summary with keywords. Rearrange the template order of your profile to highlight the most impressive and relevant pieces. *Time on task: 1–3 hrs.*

3. Network. Reach out to friends, colleagues, and acquaintances. Join Groups and send some cold-call notes, all toward the end of working your way toward that magic number: 500 connections. *Time on task: 1–2 hrs per week.*

Resources

How to Use LinkedIn: 35 Professional LinkedIn Tips for Professional Networking, Business & Marketing

blog.hubspot.com/blog/tabid/6307/bid/23454/The-Ultimate
-Cheat-Sheet-for-Mastering-LinkedIn.aspx

We covered a lot of ways to get the most out of your professional networking on LinkedIn, but it never hurts to have more advice. Here are 35 additional, solid tips for building up your profile on the leading professional networking site.

22 LinkedIn Secrets LinkedIn Won't Tell You

www.forbes.com/sites/williamarruda/2014/03/04/22
-linkedin-secrets-linkedin-wont-tell-you/#5c28943698b0

Sometimes, the best advice is not the most intuitive advice. This piece looks at some less obvious ways to maximize your time on LinkedIn. Not all of them work for everyone, so use your best judgment before doing anything rash.

New Research: 2014 LinkedIn User Trends (and 10 Top Surprises)

www.forbes.com/sites/cherylsnappconner/2014/05/04
/new-research-2014-linkedin-user-trends-and-10-top-surprises
/#3d68f5423ad2

Just as it helps to research particular industries to give you an edge over other candidates, having your finger on the pulse of the LinkedIn community's user trends can only help you in your job search.

CHAPTER EIGHT

FACEBOOK: NOT ALL FUN AND GAMES

READING TIME ⏳ 30–40 MINUTES

Who Uses Facebook?

Facebook may not seem like an obvious place to go hunting for a job. But with 60 percent of recruiters reportedly browsing the site in search of candidates—as well as apps, software programs, and professional services like Work4 Labs, Jobcast, Jobvite, and LinkUp—the platform is starting to develop an unavoidable pull in hiring and recruitment.

Here are some stats to give you a sense of Facebook's user base (per Forbes.com):

- ▶ 1.6 billion global users
- ▶ 1 billion-plus daily users
- ▶ 1.3 billion mobile users
- ▶ More than 70 percent of Facebook's users are 18 to 55 years old
- ▶ 16 million US local businesses have profiles on the network
- ▶ 75 percent of brands have Facebook pages

- 85 percent of companies with more than 100 employees use the platform
- Engagement with career pages has increased every year since their introduction

When Facebook launched in 2004, its focus was on enlarging its user base. And since it was averaging 150 million new accounts every year, growth turned out to be the least of Facebook's worries. Just over 10 years later, the company has largely switched gears, now focused on what it can do with and for the 1.6 billion users it has. On the experience end, Facebook is constantly tweaking the layout, feed hierarchy, and other features that are now familiar to about 25 percent of the world's population. They are also rolling out more features businesses can use to engage followers, including testing the waters in recruiting and employment pages. And there's a clear business imperative for Facebook to expand its professional tools. A recent report by Jobvite noted that 83 percent of users surveyed included the service as part of their job search—compared to just 36 percent for LinkedIn. Since 2013, Facebook has allowed businesses to use a feature called Career Pages—a place where they can share information on open positions and hiring practices. There are also some self-identification and search features that employers and job seekers can use to focus only on career-oriented results.

Percentage of Job Seekers Who Use These Platforms in Their Search

Facebook	83%
Twitter	40%
Google+	37%
LinkedIn	36%

While Facebook and LinkedIn differ greatly in their original purpose and uses, increasingly—and probably intentionally on Facebook's part—business and all of its attendant elements are playing a larger role in Facebook's revenue growth. This is great news for job-hunters; it means there's one more way to boost your online professional profile.

Some Work and Some Play Makes Jack a Well-Rounded Candidate

The dual focus on business and social use is creating an opportunity for Facebook users to create a hybrid identity on the service. By tweaking search results and managing lists, you can post both cat gifs *and* insightful commentary related to your career. While the overall culture of Facebook is still primarily social, by using certain settings, you can create a professional tone for specific audiences and stay up-to-date on industry information and job opportunities. Since the majority of LinkedIn users also have Facebook accounts, this can be helpful. Instead of switching back and forth between platforms, you can keep track of job opportunities, to a lesser extent, within Facebook.

Despite the growing popularity of Facebook as a job-search and recruiting platform, most people still spend their 40 minutes per day using it as it was originally intended—and that has an effect on the tone and culture of the service. Overall, users report the following reasons for using Facebook:

▶ Everyone else is on Facebook.

▶ Facebook works as an RSS reader for news.

▶ It's required to log in to other websites.

▶ You can use it to build a professional profile.

▶ Facebook groups are better than bulletin boards.

▶ It's useful for remembering birthdays.

▶ It offers a simple way to widely disseminate terrible opinions.

▶ It's an easy way to organize events.

At first glance, it might not seem like Facebook is actually that useful for job-hunters since there's only one work-specific entry on the list. But, taken as a whole, you can get a sense of how Facebook might play a role in your quest for a first, better, or new job: people use it for pretty much everything. The strength of Facebook lies in its enormity. If someone out there has a job that you want, it's a pretty safe bet that they are on the service.

Unprofessionally Professional

Back in the 1990s, there was a slate of news stories about how the Internet economy was changing the face of American business. Reputable, evergreen publishers such as the *New York Times, Forbes,* and the *Wall Street Journal* all committed pages of their periodicals to discussing and analyzing what it meant when people started showing up to work in jeans and T-shirts. Some even wondered if American business would survive. While it seems laughable now, it was the tip of an iceberg that Facebook, to a greater or lesser extent, has come to embody: a relaxed, familiar social environment.

Percentage of Recruiters Who Use These Platforms in Their Search

LinkedIn	94%
Facebook	65%
Twitter	55%
Google+	18%

Where LinkedIn has created a service that, more often than not, requires a certain respect for professionalism, Facebook is completely the opposite. Frivolity and ephemera roam free on Facebook. If LinkedIn is the workplace water cooler, Facebook is closer to the after-hours happy hour. To some extent, employers get this, and they loosen their proverbial ties to fit in on the world's largest communications network. That doesn't mean that anything goes—after all, "casual Fridays" are still workdays. It just means that companies are open to social media's relaxed environment as a venue for posting openings and finding employees. In the same way anyone using LinkedIn knows that another user might ask for help with a job search, Facebook is building out features to bridge the culture gap between the sometimes stuffy professional world and Facebook's relaxed environment.

Strengths for Job Seekers

Tweaking Facebook's features and tools to help you find a job begins with understanding how basic profile information can be used to your advantage. Here are a couple of key elements to know about.

WORK AND EDUCATION

If you have not included elements of your work history in your profile, you're missing out on a solid networking opportunity. Filling out a comprehensive work history will help your profile show up in recruiter- or software programs to search results.

PROFESSIONAL SKILLS

As with job history, the Professional Skills tab of your profile can also help potential employers find you. Facebook creates a page for a skill that a user has identified. When you choose this skill from the predetermined ones that populate the Professional Skills bar, you join everyone on Facebook who shares that skill. Recruiters and hiring managers can then search through Facebook's user base for those with specific skills.

PASSIVE CANDIDACY

Similar to LinkedIn, recruiters and hiring managers browse Facebook for passive candidates—those people with an existing job who might also be open to discussing new opportunities. While passive candidacy is less of a consideration on Facebook than on LinkedIn, filling out your work history and professional skills gives you a better chance of getting noticed by a recruiter.

SEGMENT YOUR FRIENDS

Depending on how many friends you have (the average is 338), segmenting them can be a time-consuming, but ultimately worthwhile exercise. Group friends into specific categories: family, high school friends, and, of course, colleagues and professional connections. Once you create a new group, you can change your feed settings to see only updates from that group—or post messages specifically for them. This is where you can really create multiple personalities for your Facebook profile: one for sharing cat gifs, one for videos of people falling down at weddings, one for your professional life, and so on.

GROUPS

As with LinkedIn, Facebook lets users create groups around a common interest. Sometimes, these can be hilarious—like Boobquake, a group that formed to prove that boobs do not cause earthquakes after an Iranian cleric publically claimed they did. Other times, they can be exactly what your job search needs. While some groups are closed, meaning you'll have to "friend" the creator and get an invite, others are public, meaning you can join them at will. Considering the scale of Facebook, if you do some searching, odds are you'll find what you're looking for. If you don't find the group you want, start it!

COMPANY NETWORKING SEARCH

With 1.6 billion users, there are probably more than a few people on Facebook that can help you move the needle on your job search. For example, if you really want a job at Facebook, search for everyone who has identified themselves as an employee of the company under "Work." Or, search your friend's lists by where they work. One really cool option, once you find a friend that works at the company you want to join, is searching for friends-of-friends that work at the company. The friends-of-friends networking option is a job-search goldmine.

PAGES AND CAREER PAGES

Businesses you're targeting are very likely to have an account page that you can follow. By "Liking" the page, you'll receive whatever updates the company puts out, as well as any information it shares. Liking a company page as part of your job search is an easy way to stay on top of what that company thinks is important. Where Pages will give you general information about companies, their Career Pages will give you, you guessed it, specific information about open positions. Following Pages and Career Pages is a lot easier than reminding yourself to check the company's website every day.

Weaknesses for Job Seekers

Here's where Facebook starts to bog down as a job-search tool.

CULTURE

Facebook is still primarily a social site, which means not everyone using it will be open to receiving job-related solicitations. In fact, they might even say, "Hit me up on LinkedIn for that kind of stuff." However, as Facebook moves to make room for professional culture, this may change. Facebook is taking a big step toward work utility by releasing a new service called Facebook at Work, a collaboration tool likely similar to Slack or Basecamp. And while it may take a little while to get people used to Facebook as part of day-to-day business, the company is certainly pushing in that direction.

SCALE

Facebook is clogged with advertising. Considering it is the single largest communications channel on the planet and very friendly to advertisers and revenue generated by ads essentially keeps the lights on, this should come as no surprise. As with LinkedIn, Facebook is suffering from a glut of poor-quality content created by users and services touting their "expertise" and "insight." When trying to carve out a space for yourself, make sure you're not repeating the same old information that's already been shared a thousand times.

INTERFACE

Facebook's interface can be a bit clunky to use. But that seems to be the necessary price users pay for its ubiquity. Networking on Facebook just isn't the same streamlined process that it is on LinkedIn. While searching for groups or people who work for specific companies can be a frustrating process, keep in mind that Facebook is an entirely free service, unlike LinkedIn, and you can contact as many people as you want.

Make Your Profile a Lean, Mean Referral Machine

And now for the good stuff: How to tweak your profile to help you get a job, new job, or dream job. A lot of this might be familiar, since you'll be presenting yourself as you would on LinkedIn; professionally. However, since Facebook is less focused on job searching and professional networking, you'll need less material upfront and you have to spend more time tweaking the language of your profile.

Before you start, you'll need some work-related materials on hand; it's way easier to get this stuff done ahead of time and cut and paste it into your profile than it is to type it out as you go.

Once you have all these elements together, you're ready to optimize your profile. The following tips are based on best practices related to searches, keywords, and other Facebook rules.

Facebook Profile Checklist

WORK HISTORY	Facebook provides multiple sections where you can write a truncated description of any past jobs you've had. It's best to summarize each in a line or two. You'll want to pack as many keywords as you can into these.
BACKGROUND IMAGE	Your profile has a 851 × 315 pixel banner. Make sure whatever image you upload is not controversial in any way whatsoever.
PORTRAIT	You get a minimum 180 × 180 pixel head shot. Again, make sure it's business kosher.
LINKS TO PERSONAL WEBSITES AND BLOGS	You don't need to do much with this; just cut and paste your URLs.
EDUCATION	Facebook will group you with any other alumni also on the service.
INTRO	This is a very brief summary about who you are. Be yourself—but maybe a cleaner and nicer version.

PRO TIP #1: CUSTOMIZE YOUR PROFILE URL

While it may be more aesthetic than anything else, customizing your profile URL does help with the overall professional presentation you want to stick to. Once signed into your account, go to www.facebook .com/username, and you'll see something like this:

Change the URL to your name, personal website, or something similarly appropriate.

PRO TIP #2: USE KEYWORDS WISELY

Recruiters and hiring managers search for candidates based on the words they use in their summary, work history, professional skills, and other areas of their profile. When adding keywords to your profile, it's important not to overdo it; Facebook's algorithms are pretty adept at filtering out profiles that are too keyword heavy.

PRO TIP #3: GET AS MANY CONNECTIONS AS POSSIBLE

There's really no limit to how many "friends" you should have as far as a job search goes. It probably goes without saying that, the bigger your pool of friends, the better your chances. The only downside of having more connections is a cluttered feed. To be most efficient, focus on people in your geographic area who work in fields directly related to the career you're seeking. Since the average number of Facebook users has more than 300 friends, you can benefit from exponential growth: 300 (your network) × 300 (each of your friend's networks) = 90,000 contacts.

PRO TIP #4: ADD AN APPROPRIATE PICTURE AND BACKGROUND IMAGE

Like your LinkedIn profile, if you don't have a professional-looking picture, recruiters and hiring managers are far more likely to pass you over.

Platform Etiquette

Once your profile is looking professional and optimized for recruiters and hiring managers, it's time to start mining Facebook for networking connections. As with LinkedIn, the most straightforward way to do this is to trim your contacts into a subset that work in the industry you're targeting. Then, trim the list further to include the people that do the job you want (or work with those that do). After that, it's as simple as sending polite, professional notes.

Unlike LinkedIn, Facebook makes it easy to connect with people; all you need to do is find them and click the "Add Friend" button. If you have friends in common, odds are good that they'll accept your request. There are a few other options for expanding your networking opportunities as well:

1. **Message people.** Unlike LinkedIn, you can message as many people as you want—and you don't have to be connected to them to do so. If you're using Facebook to build a professional network, it's not a bad idea to use the messaging option as a way to introduce yourself, rather than simply sending a friend request. Sending a message gives you the opportunity to put your request in context, as well as showcase your voice and personality.

2. **Join a group.** Groups are an underrated feature on Facebook. Find ones that are well populated and related to your career path, and you'll be able to leverage the group's professional connections to your advantage. Just make sure you participate for a little while before you start asking people for job referrals.

3. **Cold call.** You can build your network by finding people you think will be able to further your cause and simply clicking the "Add Friend" button. But doing so, while not necessarily viewed as unprofessional, could be taken as the equivalent of walking into someone's office, uninvited, and making yourself comfortable. It might get you some attention—but it also might not be the kind of attention you want.

Since Facebook is considered more of a social network than a professional one, there can be a temptation to go the informal route. Don't. When contacting anyone, even close friends, it's best to keep things professional.

What's an Appropriate Tone for Job Searching on Facebook?

NO	NO	YES
"Hey! I need a job . . . "	"Dear Madam, I am writing to enquire . . . "	"Ms. Chen, I've been an account manager . . . "

As with LinkedIn, the tone and frequency of your communications on Facebook are important, but they're not the only considerations. Here are a few things to keep in mind when using Facebook to boost your online profile.

TAKE IT EASY

When you're asking people to take time out of their day to share their knowledge, you don't want to seem insistent. If someone you know doesn't get back to you after a first contact, try following up a few days later. If they don't follow up with you on the second contact, you should probably drop it. If you don't know someone personally, you get one shot. If they don't respond, it's probably because they don't want to. That's okay.

BE ACTIVE

A big part of boosting your online profile is staying on the radar of recruiters and potential employers. If you never say anything, no one will ever hear you. This is not to say you should flood your feed with meaningless nonsense, but you should try to post informative material that is relevant to your industries of choice pretty regularly. As on LinkedIn, one handy way to keep your feed interesting is to summarize in a couple of lines the takeaway of whatever article, diagram, or video you're sharing.

BREVITY IS BEAUTIFUL

Clarity and brevity are important for your Facebook communication. Just like in real life, it's safe to assume that everyone is busy. Spare your would-be contacts the opus, and get to the point in a way that is clear, friendly, and concise.

Tips for Getting Hired

There are a handful of tools Facebook has that its social media counterparts simply don't. Get a handle on them and use them to your advantage.

GET FAMILIAR WITH GRAPH SEARCH

Graph Search is one of the tools that advertisers, recruiters, and brands use to target the right customer on Facebook. Recruiters and hiring managers use it to narrow down their search parameters via a variety of criteria, such as location, age, industry, and work experience. Familiarizing yourself with how Graph Search works will help you get a sense of how potential employers might find you.

COWORKER SEARCH

The utility of Coworker Search is pretty self-explanatory: it lets you easily drill down into lists of your friends who work at specific companies. To use it, click the Friends tab on you profile page (not on your home page).

Then, click on the "Find Friends" button.

On the right-hand side of your profile page, there will be a section titled Search For Friends. Toward the bottom, there will be an "Employer" option. Type in the name of the company you want to work for, and anyone in your friends-of-friends network will pop up. Friend away and start networking.

MUTUAL FRIEND SEARCH

Again, pretty self-explanatory: The Mutual Friend search helps you find mutual friends. In the same area as the Employer search, look for the section titled Mutual Friend. Enter the name of someone well connected in the industry you want to work in, and all of their connections will populate. Commence networking round 2.

We've looked at a lot of ways you can turn the big, blue time suck that is Facebook into a tool for adding another dimension to your online persona. In the next chapter, we'll look at using the job-seeking powers of another bastion of distraction: Twitter.

GET IT DONE

1. Set up your Facebook account. If you haven't already, add job summaries, education, a professional profile photo, and a work-relevant background image—not to mention links to personal websites and blogs. ⃠ *Time on task: 1 hr.*
2. Optimize your Facebook profile but customizing your profile URL and tastefully integrating pertinent keywords into your copy. ⃠ *Time on task: 1 hr.*
3. Create as big of a network in your field of interest as possible. Do some serious, targeted searching, and friend away. ⃠ *Time on task: 1–2 hrs per week.*

Resources

The Social Recruitment Monitor

www.socialrecruitmentmonitor.com/

The Social Recruitment Monitor is a site that tracks the activity of major companies as it relates to recruitment on social media. If you have a few companies in mind, it only helps to know which networks they're scouring.

The Rise of Facebook Recruiting

linkhumans.com/blog/rise-facebook-recruitment

With more than 1.6 billion Facebook users, it's no wonder that recruiters are increasingly turning their attention to the service as a way to find qualified candidates. As a job seeker, it can't hurt to get inside the head of someone using the service to find people to fill vacancies.

Five Great Examples of Companies Doing Facebook Recruiting Right

blog.capterra.com/examples-companies-facebook-recruiting/

Just because a lot of companies are using Facebook to vet potential recruits doesn't mean everyone is doing it successfully. Here's a piece on a handful of companies who excel at mining the social network for top talent.

CHAPTER NINE

TWITTER:
YOUR VOICE, YOUR TRIBE

READING TIME ⏳ 30–40 MINUTES

Who Uses Twitter?

Twitter might not know how to make any money—and Wall Street might continue to fret over that fact—but, as far as its 302 million users are concerned, that doesn't matter. Twitter is here to stay. According to CNBC, it has $3.5 billion on hand and a burn rate that says it can take 412 years to figure out how to turn a profit. Which may get you thinking, "Good for them, but what about me?"

Twitter's relevance to your job search lies in its features and operating structure. It is an incredibly efficient and cost-effective way to share up-to-the-minute information with audiences of scale. International corporations, news organizations, celebrities, small businesses, and average Joes all take advantage of the platform to share short text communications, links, photos, and videos on topics as varied as political unrest to job openings at the local coffee shop.

Here are some stats to give you a sense of Twitter's user base.

- ► 391 million accounts
- ► 302 million monthly users
- ► The number one social media channel for brand engagement
- ► 80 percent of users are on mobile
- ► 500 million tweets per day
- ► 62 percent of Twitter users are between the ages of 18 and 49
- ► Asia/Pacific enjoys the largest user base
- ► More than half of Twitter users earn $50,000-plus

Twitter, with its peer-to-peer publishing architecture, is an unparalleled social sharing and organizational tool. With a user base that overwhelmingly engages via mobile devices, it also provides a distinctly immediate and personal user experience. Brands and businesses are still experimenting with how best to take advantage of the service's unique features to drive sales, engagement, customer service, and, most important for our purposes, recruitment.

An Open Network

Twitter has a bit of a steeper learning curve, at least initially, than do more profile-based platforms like Facebook or LinkedIn. For starters, the service limits the length of messages—tweets—to 140 characters, a constraint that favors sharing links to outside information more than lengthy pieces of native writing. This brevity can be a double-edged sword: tweet-length limits make replies more likely—in fact, according to *Business Insider*, 68 percent of tweets receive replies—and make the platform itself almost inherently social. But the fact that Twitter users share more, smaller pieces of information than those on other social networks can make it harder to stand out and attract attention—something you should keep in mind when using it to network, share information, or grow a following.

Despite length limits, Twitter does make it very easy to connect with other users. Unlike LinkedIn or Facebook, there's no approval needed to follow anyone; you just find the person you're looking for and click the "Follow" button. The service's open architecture means that you can build a large pool of potential employers or thought leaders in your career area very quickly. The ability to follow whoever you want, whenever you want, gives Twitter a leg up on the other social networks in terms of building an informative, insightful network.

Strengths for Job Seekers

Using Twitter to help you find your next job involves hacking the service's features to your ends. Here are a couple of key elements to know about, as well as what you can do with them.

PROFILE

When it comes to putting together a profile, Twitter is about as easy as it gets. Compared with Facebook and LinkedIn, Twitter certainly doesn't depend on extracting nearly as much personal information from its users and sharing it with advertisers. Upon sign-up, you're asked for all of seven things:

1. A header photo
2. A profile photo
3. Username
4. Bio (160-character limit)
5. Location
6. Personal website URL
7. Birthday

Oh, and you get to choose your Twitter theme color.

PASSIVE CANDIDACY

As with other social media sites, recruiters and hiring managers use Twitter to search for and vet passive candidates. It's a good idea to build an account that reflects your professional side. Remember, 55 percent of recruiters note that they use Twitter to search for candidates. Don't give anyone a reason to hit the reject button on your candidacy before it even begins.

FOLLOWING AND BEING FOLLOWED

At its most basic, there are two things you can do on Twitter: follow people or be followed. Whenever someone you follow tweets something, it will show up in your feed. And, you guessed it, whenever you tweet something, it will show up in your followers' feeds. While it may seem pretty basic, there are a number of ways you can make it work for you.

LISTS

Since Twitter's design favors sharing small bits of information, even a small list of users will generate a steady stream of tweets. This can get overwhelming pretty quickly, especially if you're using the service for both professional and personal use. To help manage the flow of information, you can group people you follow and people who follow you together. For example, if you want to see only what your "Business Tax Accounting" list is up to, just click on that list and your feed will show only what the people in the list have shared.

You have the option to make your lists "public" or "private." Only you have access to private lists, but anyone who follows you has access to a public list. At first glance, public lists might not seem like they add a lot of value to the service, but, depending on how much work you put into them, they can be a big help in establishing your reputation. If you put time and effort into finding a list of sources that constantly provide experienced, insightful information on a subject or business, you've essentially created a feed for other people to follow. Done well, a public list can attract a lot of followers to your account. On the other side of the same coin, you can pretty easily take advantage of lists that other people may have already artfully curated.

SEARCH

As with everything online, Twitter is keyword searchable. This is hugely important to recognize for two reasons: (1) it is how you will find people you want to connect with and jobs you want to apply for within the service, and (2) it is also how recruiters will find you on the service (and sometimes outside of it). When setting up your profile, choose two or three keywords to work into your description; make sure they are consistent with your other social media accounts for maximum benefit.

Beyond keywords, searching on Twitter is built around the # and @ symbols. Hashtags (#) are used to identify keywords in a tweet and group those keywords together throughout the service. You can click on a hashtagged word or phrase to see all posts with that same hashtag. For instance, if you clicked on #jobs (or typed it into the search bar), every single tweet or profile where that hashtag appears would be at your fingertips. Of course, using hugely broad hashtags like #jobs will likely give you an impossible amount of information to comb through. The more specific you can be, the better, in terms of focusing your search (and tagging your own content).

The @ symbol is used to reply to or address someone directly. People use this to start conversations with each other or to call people's attention to a particular tweet. It's important to remember, though, that this conversation is hardly private; it will show up in your feed, as well as the feeds of *all of your followers.*

Know Your # from Your @

Sometimes people confuse # and @ and use them interchangeably, particularly when they're just getting started. Make sure you understand the difference; misusing a tool is certainly not going to be attractive to recruiters or potential employers.

The # is how you'll be able to establish your proficiency, expertise, and insight on a certain subject. People who search for specific hashtags will come to associate your username with whatever it is they're searching for. Considering how many people use the service professionally, you probably won't be able to "own" any one hashtag. But the more you use it and the more quality tweets you share with that hasthag, the greater your association with it will be.

Using @ can draw another user's attention to something you've posted. This can be helpful when trying to build a network of potential employers. Like anything, you don't want to abuse it. If you @ someone too much, even if you're trying to get them to follow you, they may end up blocking you because you're an annoyance. So, use it sparingly, when you really feel like you're contributing to a conversation.

DIRECT MESSAGES

To accommodate private conversations, Twitter has a feature called direct messages (DM). You can send anyone who follows you a direct message or create a list of people to send a message to. While anyone in the list can respond and partake in the conversation, they must be following you for them to receive the message. Of course, there are exceptions; some individuals, and thankfully a lot of businesses, adjust their settings so that anyone can send them a DM. Before you do this yourself, do some soul searching. While it makes it easier for anybody to get in touch with you, it also opens you up to spam in a serious way.

Weaknesses for Job Seekers

Twitter's strength lies in its open networking—you can follow anyone, and by doing so open up the potential for a conversation—and in its professional user base. Of course, it's not perfect. Here's where you might run into problems using it in your job search.

LIMITED SHARING

It's quite possible that, by the time this book has been printed and distributed, Twitter will have made some major changes to its basic operating features and this paragraph will be moot. At present, though, Twitter is not very good at sharing rich content. For example, if you find an article on trends shaping the veterinary medical supply business, you can only briefly summarize why you're sharing it—140 characters max, including the link to the article. So, it's not a great place for nuanced, complex insight. If they end up increasing the character max, that could change.

SCALE

Twitter is the smallest of the major social media channels. But it makes up for its size by boasting a concentrated professional network and an engaged user base.

AN EMBARRASSMENT OF RICHES

Since there are arguably no rules about who uses which hashtags to tag what kind of content, searching for job feeds and professional organizations can be a bit messy. For example, searching for "jobs" or "#jobs" brings up every tweet with the word in it—everything from news stories to people griping about their day-to-day work to actual job postings. While the postings might be in there, you'll probably have to do a whole lot of searching to find them.

Polish Your Profile

Twitter's sparse architecture can be both a good and bad thing for job seekers. On one hand, unlike LinkedIn, you don't have many oppor-tunities to load your profile up with keywords in order to land on the radar of recruiting apps and hiring manager searches. On the other hand, Twitter's bare-bones interface keeps its users honest. Sure, you can throw some keywords or hashtags into the 160 characters you get for a bio. But if you want to get the most out of your time on Twitter, you'll really have to do it the old-fashioned way and work for it.

You won't need much to set up your profile; creating your account, if you don't already have one, shouldn't take more than five minutes.

Unlike the other social media services, you don't gain much by optimizing your profile to show up in recruiter-software searches. It's how you use Twitter that will help with your job search; the account by itself will do nothing for you.

Twitter Etiquette: Tweet Like a Pro

Etiquette on Twitter is more about using the platform's features and tools correctly than anything else. As a rule of thumb, it's best not to use more than two hashtags in any one post. Why? With so few characters available in each post, you really want to save your breath for what's important. Also, Twitter can view accounts that overuse hashtags as spam accounts, sometimes shutting them down entirely or suppressing them in internal search results. It's never good to get a spam reputation online.

Twitter Profile Checklist

USERNAME	Pick something professional and personal. If available, you're probably best off going with the first letter of your first name and your last name. Otherwise, pick something that's directly related to the majority of what you'll be posting about: mediaguy, Giantsfan, accountingwhiz, etc.
BACKGROUND IMAGE	Your profile has a 1500 × 500 pixel banner. Make sure whatever image you choose to put there is not controversial in any way.
PORTRAIT	You get a minimum 400 × 400 pixel head shot. Again, make sure it's business appropriate.
LINK TO A PERSONAL WEBSITE OR BLOG	Pretty self-explanatory. Type or paste the appropriate URL here.
BIO	You get just a scant 160 characters, keywords included, so make it brief, to the point, and professional. (The text in this box is exactly 160 characters long.)

Getting the most out of networking on Twitter really comes down to sharing useful information with your followers and being selective about who you follow. You'll get more bang for your buck, grow your network faster, and burnish your reputation by concentrating on subjects specific to your career path. Here are some tips to consider when managing your daily feed.

PRIVATE VS. PUBLIC POSTS

This is pretty straightforward: if you aren't comfortable sharing something with, potentially, the entire Twittersphere, don't post it publically. Also, if you initiate a private Twitter conversation, keep it private. Don't betray that initial framework. Think about it along the lines of a secret; don't share what goes on in private posts.

Public conversations can become private ones when what's being discussed loses relevance for your followers at large. So, if you need to explain something specific or ask a question that might not benefit everyone following you, take it private; save your followers the trouble of having to sift through your extraneous back and forth.

TONE

It's probably best to reiterate the "just the facts" aspect of Twitter here. One hundred forty characters is a miniscule amount of space to provide context to something you share. If you're unsure about how people will take a post, don't post it. That said, some users are really good at expressing humor, intimacy, and other emotions on the service. Before you try your hand at slinging one-liners, study some of the best ones that you've found.

FREQUENCY

How much is too much? It's case by case. Base whether or not you post something on how useful it will be to your followers rather than how recently you tweeted. However, a dead Twitter feed can show lack of initiative. Compared to other job candidates who regularly tweet great information, a silent feed might be a differentiating factor in the eyes of potential employers or recruiters. The more quality information you tweet on subjects specific to your target industry, the better. It can't hurt to make it part of your regular job-search routine.

STAY ON TARGET

You want your Twitter feed to reinforce your engagement and knowledge of your industry. Your tweets should heavily favor work-related information. That said, including a bit of your personality and daily life is by no means taboo. Doing so can give potential employers a window into what kind of person, as well as employee, you are. Just weigh your tweets heavily on the work side of the scale.

Twitter's 140-character limit might make it seem like the service isn't professional in tone. This isn't true. Just because your messages will be short doesn't mean that you can lapse into informalities when you post. More than anything, the brevity of the platform reinforces the need to make your point quickly and clearly.

Find and Build Your Tribe

Twitter's biggest asset as far as your job search is concerned is its professional, dedicated user base. Not everyone on it uses the service for networking or insight into their industry, but those who do tend to be highly engaged. Industry people who tweet seriously are going to be more informed and willing to discuss the particulars and challenges of their business than people on some other networks. While this sets the bar a bit higher for you in terms of building a following, it also means you can find really good information relatively easily by following the right people.

With Twitter, you benefit from the experience of everyone you follow. In a very real way, they give you their sources of information. When setting up your feed, it makes sense to follow industry and thought leaders related to your field of work. Beyond following the right people, here are a few ways to get the most out of your time on Twitter.

MAKE LISTS

Creating a public list of your top sources turns your feed into a great resource for other Twitter users to follow. Not only can you benefit from the information the people you follow are sharing, but your account can gain a following because of their good work.

To set up a public list, do the following:

1. Identify the people who consistently provide insightful and useful information.
2. Hover over your profile picture at the top right of your account window.
3. Click on "Lists."

4. Click on "Create new list."
5. Write an accurate description of your list. When like-minded users search for information, your list description will impact what is returned in their search. Make sure the "Public" option is checked.

6. Then, add the users, businesses, or brands you've identified to the list. To add people to your public list, click on the gear icon next to their profile summary.

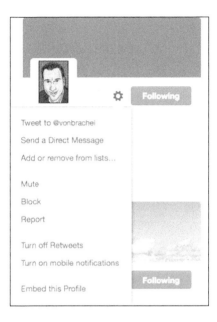

7. Choose "Add or remove from lists," and add the person to the appropriate list(s).

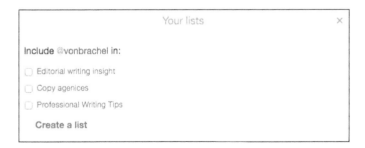

Now, anyone who comes across your profile will see the option to follow the lists you've set up.

JOB SEARCH WITH HASHTAGS

Most of the job searching you'll do on Twitter will happen through the search bar. It's pretty simple: enter the hashtags you're looking for as well as a location; otherwise, you'll get every tweet related to the more general hashtags. For example, searching #job #editor #seattle returned 10 different Tweets containing my search parameters.

While you can vary which hashtags you use to search with, here's a list of the most common hashtags employers use to identify their open positions:

- ▶ #hiring
- ▶ #jobfairy
- ▶ #employment
- ▶ #jobs
- ▶ #joblisting

- ▶ #careers
- ▶ #tweetmyjobs
- ▶ #gethired
- ▶ #jobopening
- ▶ #jobposting

FOLLOW @JOB ACCOUNTS

One of the surest ways to get Twitter to shower you with a steady supply of jobs is to create a list of the @[company name]jobs accounts for companies you'd like to work for. Almost all businesses use Twitter to promote open positions they are looking to fill. An added benefit of following company @jobs accounts is that they'll often share their public lists, including the team of employees responsible for managing the hiring. Not all companies use @jobs, so also try searching @careers, @jobpostings, @jobopenings, @hiring, and so on.

It's also a pretty good idea to follow recruiters and hiring agencies that cover your industry and to organize them into a separate list.

We've covered how the big three social media channels—LinkedIn, Facebook, and Twitter—can help you advance your job search and career. While they're the most commonly used by job seekers, recruiters, hiring managers, and employers, they are by no means the only options available to you. In the next chapter, we're going to look at a few other channels you can use to boost your online profile.

GET IT DONE

1. Set up your Twitter account, complete with a keyword-packed bio, professional profile photo, background image, and links to your personal website or blog. X *Time on task: Not much more than 5 mins.*

2. Follow people! Start with companies you'd like to work for, recruiters, hiring managers, thought leaders in your industry, and @jobs accounts. After that, build some public lists around specific professional interests. X *Time on task: 1 hr per week.*

3. Start tweeting. To get the most bang for your networking buck—and to build up a meaningful following—tweet regularly. Go easy on the hashtags, and try to stay focused on insightful information related to your targeted field(s). X *Time on task: 1–2 hrs per week.*

Resources

Three Tips for Writing a Killer Twitter Bio to Get Targeted Followers

www.adweek.com/socialtimes/3-tips-for-writing-a-killer-twitter-bio-to-get-targeted-followers/441617

While having a large following probably isn't a bad thing, it's a lot more useful in terms of job seeking—and enjoyable, in terms of interactions—if those followers share something meaningful in common with you. This piece looks at ways to attract like-minded folks with your Twitter bio—as well as a few things to avoid.

Social Media Update 2014

www.pewinternet.org/2015/01/09/social-media-update-2014/

The Pew Research Center takes a good, hard look at the major trends and forces that shape the way we live today. In this piece, they focus their attention and share their observations on social media.

How to Use Twitter to Find a Job

www.biginterview.com/blog/2015/03/twitter-jobs.html

We covered a lot of ways you can use Twitter in your job search, but it seems there are always more. This piece looks at how to use Twitter to unearth hidden job opportunities, build your personal brand, and more.

CHAPTER TEN

OTHER PLATFORMS

READING TIME ⏳ 30–40 MINUTES

Who's Left?

Just as LinkedIn, Facebook, and Twitter are all unique in their features, reach, and capabilities, so are a number of other, sometimes less explicitly, business-oriented platforms. But just because certain platforms are not commonly thought of as career oriented doesn't mean they can't be. It just means you'll have to get creative to make them work for your purposes. In this chapter, we'll look at examples of how others have used a few of these products and services to get jobs and interviews, as well as the strengths and weaknesses of each when it comes to job hunting.

Have a Home Base

The first thing a recruiter, hiring manager, or potential employer is going to do when considering you for an open position is make sure you can do the job. As a job seeker, you want to make checking that requirement off their list as convenient as possible. The best way to do this is to make examples of your work easily available. This, of course, will mean different things for people working in different industries. Creatives should have examples of their best work—whether its videos, design samples, music, or something else entirely—hosted online and, ideally, on a personal website. People working in the sciences should include published research; managers will want to share project or program accomplishments; salespeople may consider disclosing revenue earned or new account information. Whatever your area of expertise, a personal website showcasing it will clear one of the first hurdles you'll face in the eyes of prospective employers.

Websites and blogs used to be bespoke projects. Luckily for you, that's no longer the case. Services such as Squarespace, WordPress, Tumblr, and others have taken much of the technical expertise out of the equation. At minimal cost, you can now build a professional Web presence for yourself—one that hosts examples of your work and your work history and gives you a platform from which to share your ideas, insights, and thoughts about your career and industry. Probably the best argument for including some kind of personal website or blog as part of your online profile is that it gives you the opportunity to create an immersive, creative, and contextual environment that potential employers can explore—and it's all about you.

Without further ado, let's take a look at a few helpful platforms outside the big three.

Tumblr

Tumblr grew out of a mid-2000s Internet trend called microblogging. Microblogs were essentially a shortened, Internet-friendly version of blogging. If you didn't want to commit to writing multi-thousand word essays—or reading them—microblogs encouraged you to just write shorter versions. Additionally, Tumblr lets you post videos, images, music, links, quotes, and whatever else catches your interest. Aside from brevity, Tumblr's big differentiator is that it added a social layer to the platform. Other account holders can follow your blog, like what you share, comment on it, and repost your posts on their own pages.

If this sounds like Facebook, that's because, conceptually speaking, it's not all that different. However, the service does not force you to use a one-size-fits-all template. You can customize your account with different theme colors, images, layouts, and other options.

Tumblr Quick Stats

SIZE	USERS	BUSINESS OR PERSONAL
278 million pages	Teens to young adults	Personal

CAN IT HELP ME FIND A JOB?

In a roundabout way, yes, Tumblr may be able to help you find a job. Tumblr is popular with fandom culture—people who create websites and blogs in appreciation of TV shows, movies, celebrities, products, and anything else worthy of fawning over. You may be able to glean good insight and research from what its users are posting, and you can interact with those users.

BEST PRACTICES

Tumblr (and WordPress, Squarespace, Wix, Weebly, and many other services) will prompt you to add keywords at various stages of the building process. Make sure that the keywords you choose are specific to the jobs that you will be applying for—and that they are consistent across your online channels, from LinkedIn to Twitter and Facebook. The more specific keywords you can attribute to yourself throughout your profile channels, the better the results will be. You should also regularly be working these keywords into your posts. Remember, Google search results, as well as recruiting software, are always looking for keywords; you can amplify them by consistently using the same ones when putting your insight and thoughts online.

Wordpress

WordPress is a platform for building websites, as well as a personal blogging service. To get a bit more technical, it is an "online, open-source website-creation tool written in PHP." Just as a house is built on a foundation, a lot of websites are built on WordPress's underlying code. The service is popular with both businesses and individuals looking to create content-rich sites.

WordPress Quick Stats

SIZE	USERS	BUSINESS OR PERSONAL
More than 75 million websites use WordPress; WordPress accounts for over 25% of all websites and over 50% of all content management websites	Everyone from independent bloggers to major brands.	Both

CAN IT HELP ME FIND A JOB?

Yes, especially if you are interested in marketing, communications, coding, design, or anything that might involve knowledge of a company's website. An attractive, elegant WordPress site stands as its own example of work. There are no social capabilities to network around, but you can build social feeds into WordPress sites.

BEST PRACTICES

Make sure that your website is linked to your social media channels and vice versa. Doing so will make it easier for a potential employer or recruiter to find all of the things that you want them to see. Linking them all together will help a hiring manager or potential boss find everything in one place when it comes time to vet you. Personal websites tend to rank fairly high in Google searches; sites with links will get seated even higher up in the results.

Squarespace

Like its competitors Weebly and Wix, Squarespace is a paid service that lets you build a personal website fairly easily using predesigned templates. The company is focused on providing customers with personal or small business websites on a subscription basis.

Squarespace Quick Stats

SIZE	USERS	BUSINESS OR PERSONAL
1.8 million websites	Individuals, small businesses, and large companies.	Both

WILL IT HELP ME FIND A JOB?

Not in and of itself, but as a channel for building your online profile and showcasing your work, Squarespace is a good option.

BEST PRACTICES

If you're going to take the trouble to build a website or blog, you should make sure it's above board. If you use images and art, which you absolutely should, make sure that they're either yours or are rights free (e.g., in the public domain) or that you have paid the appropriate licensing fees. Additionally, it's a really good idea to run your copy by an editor to make sure that there are no grammatical, factual, or logical errors. Nobody likes a dummy; potential employers may even reject you if your website contains spelling and grammar errors. If that potential employer is Google, they definitely will.

Instagram

Instagram is a social media channel that lets users share pictures and videos with one another and reshare images within the service. Additionally, users can briefly comment on one another's accounts. Facebook bought them for $1.3 billion in 2012 as a way to grow and solidify its mobile-market share, as well as provide a larger mobile audience to its advertisers.

Instagram Quick Stats

SIZE	USERS	BUSINESS OR PERSONAL
300+ million	Teens to young adults	Both

WILL IT HELP ME FIND A JOB?

Yes, with qualifications. Instagram's popularity and rapidly growing user base means that it's a channel that shouldn't be ignored. This is especially true for photographers, filmmakers, and any other creatives. Additionally, the largely under-30 user base means that anyone looking to advance a career in business focused on younger people cannot overlook Instagram's importance. It's a primary channel of communication for teens, young adults, and, increasingly, middle-aged folks.

One of Instagram's greatest assets is its popularity with businesses: more than 85 percent of major world brands use the service to communicate with their customers. For whatever reason, user engagement with companies active on Instagram is 58 times higher than Facebook and 122 times higher than those on Twitter. This means that a lot of businesses are very active on the platform, sharing tons of information via their accounts, including job openings.

Instagram has flown under the radar as far as job-search channels go, but the practice is growing, especially for small and local businesses. The reason is pretty simple: there are more than 70 million

Instagram users in the United States, and placing a job posting is free. But it's not just small businesses that are doing it. Big companies have taken to the practice simply because it's too big a talent pool to ignore.

BEST PRACTICES

All of the professional rules of etiquette apply to Instagram. You'll need to load your account with keywords where relevant and refrain from any of the no-nos: swearing, racism, misogyny, sexism, etc. Basically, keep it professional. And don't be an asshole.

The search function on Instagram is less for the job seeker and more for the recruiter. You might find your dream job posted there, but it's not likely. There are hundreds of millions of posts uploaded to the service every day, making it pretty much impossible to wade through them all. But a recruiter might be searching for someone with your skills—skills you've likely tagged your posts with. (#amirite?) As with Twitter and other social media channels, you can tag and search using the # symbol. This means that you can share your work, particularly if it's conducive to visual representation, and tag it with relevant terms, i.e., #UX, #CPA, #mechanic, #design, etc.

As on the big three platforms, you can follow companies that you want to work for. If they post a job opening to their Instagram account, you'll be notified. Setting up an Instagram account specifically for the purpose of following companies you want to work for, be they local or national, will make it easier for you to keep track of who's posting what. More important, it will give you a different kind of insight into those companies.

Using Instagram as a source of information about a company or business you want to work for is not so much about studying their marketing materials (unless, of course, you're in marketing) so much as it is about what employees will share on their personal accounts. You'll get insight into a company's culture, what the actual workspace looks like, when events happen, and a whole host of other off-the-grid information.

How Instagram Helped One Candidate Land a Job

Aja Frost used Instagram in an unconventional way—and it gave her an edge over other applicants, as well as helped her figure out what to say during the interview process. Here's what she did.

STEP 1: Make a list of all the companies you want to work for and follow them on Instagram. Not all companies are easy to find within the service itself, but Google makes this part pretty easy: Just Google "company name" + "Instagram," and, most likely, it will be the first result that comes up.

STEP 2: Go to LinkedIn and search for employees who work at the company, ideally in the department you want to work for. You guessed it, Google "employee name" + "Instagram." It may take a few tries to get the right person, but all you need is a few people to follow. Once you find a couple of people, look to see if they've tagged other employees in group shots. Follow them as well.

STEP 3: See if you can find a picture in the office that an employee has geotagged. Click on that geotag and it will bring up every picture on Instagram at that location.

STEP 4: Start looking for trends in the pictures, such as days of the week or month when the company has events, outings, or celebrations or buys the employees lunch. The more you browse, the better idea you'll have of what it's like to work there—and ultimately if it's a good fit for you. This was where Aja hit pay dirt. She noticed that Braintree bought its employees tacos every Tuesday and brought up the "Taco Tuesday" phenomenon during her interview. It broke down the formalities and opened up a much more relaxed conversation. With that ace up her sleeve, she got the position.

Pinterest

Pinterest is essentially an online, sharable bookmarking service. I know, it sounds weird.

How does it work? Users find things online they like—pretty much anything, from recipes to humor, DIY, and crafts—and "pin" them to their account board (feed). Pins get grouped together based on keywords denoting their subject, and users can search through these groupings, or pin boards, to find similar items that they're interested in. Users can also like, comment on, or share pinned items.

Pinterest's popularity stems from its requirement that whatever is pinned must be visual: a photo, illustration, design, video, and so on. You can't share text or links. Brands are particularly interested in Pinterest because users pin and share an enormous number of products on the site. Those products get grouped on boards, allowing consumers to discuss their relative merits and weaknesses. The market research focus of the site is a by-product of its original intent but a boon to businesses nonetheless.

Pinterest Quick Stats

SIZE	USERS	BUSINESS OR PERSONAL
50+ million	Teens to young adults	Personal

WILL IT HELP ME FIND A JOB?

Sort of. While Pinterest is probably the weakest social media channel for explicitly searching for jobs, it does attract a lot of interest from businesses. There are a number of job- and career-related pin boards on the site, but they don't differ all that much in function from more traditional sites like Monster. You can use it to network and research brands and companies you want to work for in much the same way you'd use any other social media service: Comment on other people's pins, share your own, be professional, and so on.

BEST PRACTICES

Because of its heavy focus on visuals, Pinterest is a great service to showcase any part of your career related to imagery: photos, videos, physical products, data visualization, infographics, and other design samples. The more beautiful the image, the more it will get shared, noticed, and commented on. If you are producing stellar imagery, then absolutely sign up and share away.

Another way to put Pinterest to work for you is to rethink what a job history should be. Rather than type out blurbs describing past experience like you might on LinkedIn or Facebook, break up your work history into visual, image-rich components. Divide your bio, education, and job descriptions into individual pins, rich with eye-catching graphic content. If nothing else, it will show initiative and an unconventional way of representing yourself.

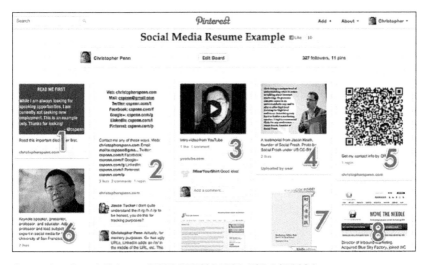

Source: farm8.staticflickr.com/7052/6776954524_535ab05038.jpg

Lastly, pin boards are great ways to curate information on a subject. There are a ton of career advice experts and businesses using Pinterest to share insight into their respective areas of expertise. Benefit from their efforts. For example, the job service CareerBliss manages a pin board they regularly update with news and trends around a host of industries, as well as government data about employment. Play around with the service's search function. You should be able to find a couple of relevant resources fairly quickly.

YouTube

For those who've been living in the woods without electricity or an Internet connection for the last decade, YouTube is a portal for hosting, sharing, and commenting on video content. Google bought the service in 2006 for $1.65 billion as a long-term investment, betting that consumers would increasingly turn to the Internet for video-based content. While it sounds obvious now, at the time many business experts thought the purchase would never pay off, concerned that television would remain the preferred media channel for video and that, like Napster, YouTube would fall prey to copyright-infringement lawsuits.

YouTube Quick Stats

SIZE	USERS	BUSINESS OR PERSONAL
1 billion+	Everyone, but skews young	Both

The initial vision for the site was that people would upload and share their own content—a DIY community of video and filmmaker enthusiasts. Presently, the site receives four billion views *every single day,* raking in more than $4 billion annually in revenue.

There is also a social element to the service. Users can share videos to their other social media channels, create playlists, comment, and subscribe to other users, channels. While YouTube is pretty limited compared to other social media platforms, what it lacks in features, it makes up for in use. YouTube is the only social media service that rivals Facebook in size and engagement.

WILL IT HELP ME FIND A JOB?

As with Instagram, companies and small businesses often share job openings on YouTube, but there is no simple way to find those openings without wading through lots of irrelevant material. While you can subscribe to the channels of companies you'd like to work for to receive notifications when new videos and announcements are uploaded, YouTube's overall utility as a job board is fairly limited. That said, the sheer size of YouTube's user base makes it difficult for companies to completely ignore the channel.

BEST PRACTICES

The first thing you'll want to do is make a list of the companies you'd like to work for and subscribe to their YouTube channels. Set your notifications to alert you whenever a new video or announcement is uploaded and shared by your potential employer. Most large corporations use multiple channels to highlight specific arms of their business—including career channels. GE, for example, created a channel called "GE Careers" that hosts dozens of videos related to working at GE.

Like Pinterest and Instagram, YouTube is also a pretty good place to read up on companies you're targeting. Large businesses, like the aforementioned GE, churn out millions of dollars' worth of customer-focused marketing content about themselves. It's worth browsing these videos to get an idea of what they might be looking for in employees, where they are making strategic bets, and what kind of culture the company represents. Watching the videos can be very helpful during the interview processes or while networking with the company's hiring managers on other sites.

And of course, if you work directly with video, there's an obvious reason for you to use YouTube (and other similar sites, like Vimeo). Use the site to promote yourself—through trailer-length versions of videos you've shot or personal bio videos where you share your insight and experience. Just be careful; doing so can be a dicey undertaking. Remember Aleksey Vayner and the blowback of his "Impossible Is Nothing" video, trying to court UBS? Tread lightly—and make sure you ask a few people to look over anything that could be potentially humiliating before you share it with the world.

So far, we've talked about ways to build up your online profile and use a number of existing platforms to your advantage. In the next chapter, we'll look at perhaps the most effective and powerful way to put yourself a few handshakes from getting hired: networking.

GET IT DONE

1. Put together a personal website or blog. Be sure it links to all of your social media accounts. Remember, you want to make it easy on recruiters, so put everything in one place. If money is an object, some platforms don't cost a nickel; start there. *☒ Time on task: 1–4 hrs.*

2. Set up accounts on Tumblr, Instagram, and whichever other platforms might be useful for your particular industry. If you're in video, don't miss YouTube and Vimeo. If you're in design, don't overlook Pinterest. Do what's right for you. Just be sure the image you're projecting is consistent with the material you put out on other channels. *☒ Time on task: 1–2 hrs.*

3. Use some of the "minor" platforms to get a fuller picture of companies you're trying to court. Doing this kind of homework can really pay off, particularly if you make it to in-person interviews. *☒ Time on task: 1–2 hrs per week.*

Resources

Social Media Demographics to Inform a Better Segmentation Strategy

sproutsocial.com/insights/new-social-media-demographics/

This piece takes a deep dive into the demographics of many social media platforms, presenting findings in an accessible and largely visual way. Keep your finger on the pulse to make sure you're spending your online time as productively as possible.

A Long List of Instagram Statistics and Facts (That Prove Its Importance)

blog.hootsuite.com/instagram-statistics-for-business/

If, after reading this chapter, you're not completely sold on where Instagram fits into your job-seeking online life, you probably will be after reading this.

Eight Pinterest Statistics That Marketers Can't Ignore

sproutsocial.com/insights/pinterest-statistics/

If you're stuck on a caricature of Pinterest as "that place moms go to find sewing patterns and recipes," you're really doing yourself a disservice. Particularly if you work (or would like to work) in marketing, ignore Pinterest at your peril.

CHAPTER ELEVEN

GROW YOUR NETWORK

READING TIME ⏳ 30–40 MINUTES

It's All About Who You Know

Truer words were rarely spoken. While "who you know" used to refer to the Old Boys' Club, its present meaning has shifted to describe a more benign phenomenon in the job-hunter's life. The simple truth about finding a job, your next job, or your dream job is that it will depend on your ability to do the work, your fit within a company's culture, and, most importantly, your professional network.

To be clear, knowing the right people doesn't mean generating a list of personal relations that you can manipulate into advancing your career, relying on nepotism to get hired, or cultivating power players to gain access to their influence. Networking is fundamentally about being involved, being on call, and spreading a good professional reputation. All of the platforms and strategies we've discussed in this book so far ultimately wind up supporting this most important of practices.

In this chapter, we'll look at some of the best ways to grow your personal network.

How Positions Get Filled

Taking for granted that you're only applying for jobs you are qualified for, the single most beneficial thing you can do is grow your network as large as it can be. Even so, a huge number of jobs—somewhere between 50 percent and 80 percent, depending on who you ask—get filled without ever being publicized. Why? A few reasons.

The first is simply the fact that people trust people they already know more than people they don't. If you've worked with someone and respect them, odds are you'll take their recommendation over a stranger's any day. "First thing I do is ask around the office if they know someone who'd be a good fit for the job," Ryan Woodring says.

The second reason is that it's a lot less work to fill a job by word-of-mouth—and its attendant-filtering process—than it is to wade through the average 120 applications every public job opening receives. Woodring continues, "Most of the time I find someone that way, and never mess with LinkedIn or posting a position."

And finally, sometimes hiring managers are looking to replace an existing employee who might be underperforming. "You'd have to be stupid to publically announce you're going to fire someone months before you get around to doing it," notes Joan Miller.

Every recruiter and hiring manager I talked to described a similar process for filling an open position.

To make your job search and career arc as efficient and successful as possible—and have a shot at positions that don't make it past stage four—it helps to be known, in a good way.

How Open Positions Get Filled

1.	Ask everyone in the department if they know a good candidate.
2.	Ask everyone in the company if they know a good candidate.
3.	Ask everyone in your personal network if they know a good candidate.
4.	Ask former coworkers or employers if they know a good candidate.
5.	Employ a professional recruiter.
6.	Recruiter looks to their past placements for a candidate.
7.	Recruiter asks their network of recruiters if they have a good candidate.
8.	Recruiter and hiring manager publicize the position.

So, Who Do You Know?

If you're on Facebook, you are fewer than four connections away from everyone else on Facebook—about one-sixth of the world's population. I raise this wowzer just to point out that you are connected to far more people than you might think.

So, what do you do with all these connections? First, find out who you know personally that works in the industry you're targeting. Ask them, politely and professionally, who they might be willing to introduce you to. Just doing that will set you up for a networking bonanza once you go online and start building connections in earnest.

Whenever you do meet someone—at a party, at a job interview, or through a project you work on—be sure to follow up with them. A quick, friendly email can be the difference between being remembered and being forgotten. Detailed follow-ups are better than generic ones, so be sure to include a few specifics about the circumstances

The Only Follow-Up Email You'll Ever Need

[Name of person],

It was great to meet you at [wherever you met]. Thanks for talking about [X,Y,Z] with me, I've been wondering about that for a while now, and your perspective helped make some sense of it.

Until next time,

[Your name]

of your meeting. It's usually better to wait for them to respond before following up on social media—the personal email is a great anchor point for other types of impersonal communication.

One thing to note is that there is a golden rule to networking: the favor economy is limitless. If helping someone out costs you nothing, do it. Hoarding your resources and connections will only constrain the growth of your own network and cloud your reputation. Asking someone for a favor doesn't put you in their pocket; all it means is that they know they can ask you for a favor in the future—and you should be happy to be in that kind of debt.

The Right Crowd

Not that long ago it would have taken years, if not decades, to compile a list of the contact information, positions, locations, past work histories, and other professional vitals of 500 people. Presently, even if you're just starting out, LinkedIn and other social media services make it possible to build your own network of that size in under a year. All things considered, that's pretty remarkable.

But quantity is not quality. Casting a wide net through your social media channels and making as many connections as possible is a good thing in the sense that it's a means to an end. You want to make as many connections as possible in order to build a solid professional network of *the right kind of people.* If that sounds elitist, hear me out for a second. The right kind of people are just like you. They will have a reputation for:

- ▶ Working hard
- ▶ Doing the job to the best of their abilities
- ▶ Being generous with their time, support, and expertise
- ▶ Helping others improve
- ▶ Being accountable

Depending on your experience level, you can add a recognized and demonstrated mastery of the skills it takes to be successful in your chosen vocation. Finding people who are generally recognized as leaders in their field is not that difficult. More difficult is finding people who are both leaders *and* willing to share their experience and connections with you. The great thing about business, work, and life is that, as a general rule, like attracts like. All you really need to do is network your way into the ambit of one person who is as generous with their experience and connections as you are, and the rest will follow.

Getting Virtually Acquainted

Finding people in your personal network who are willing to help can be as simple as asking around. Building those relationships online, however, is a different story. The first, and easiest, step is finding them. Start simply by going to LinkedIn and checking out their Influencers page. At first you're going to see a bunch of people that will in no way be willing to personally help you: Richard Branson, Deepak Chopra, David Cameron, Arianna Huffington, etc. Just keep clicking on the "See More" option underneath the head shots. Pretty soon, you'll start seeing regular people. Keep looking until you find an influencer who works in your field.

If that doesn't work, there's another fairly easy way to get connected to heavyweights in your field: type your occupation or industry into LinkedIn's search bar. It can take you all of two minutes to find

Finding Great Connections

YES	NO	
		Are they in your geographic location?
		Would you work directly with them or in their department?
		Do you know people in common who can introduce you?
		Are they sharing their thoughts, ideas, and expertise on social media?
		Do you have insight into how you can help their business/work?

Results: If you checked *Yes* more often than *No*, you should probably reach out to that person.

potential connections—or connections of connections—in your field and area. If you spend a few hours a week researching connections via social media channels, news outlets, and the ever-useful Google search page, odds are you'll turn up a few dozen people to reach out to every session.

A Strong Handshake

When I was a kid, my mom bugged the hell out of me by telling me the rules of handshaking over and over again: Look the person in the eye and say, "Hello, [their name], good to meet you." It got to the point where I felt like she was just saying it just to torture me. Forty years later, it's become a reflex. That's how you create a habit: you do it over and over again until you don't even think about it anymore.

Asking for an introduction to someone who does great work, is well respected in your field, heads a department that you really want to work in, or is just plain interesting shouldn't be that different. To make a strong impression, both with people you're asking a favor of and people you've never met before, it helps to have a practiced, familiar, and polite routine.

As noted earlier, you should start building your network within your existing professional circle. If someone you know knows someone you want to know, there are a couple of ways you can go about asking for an introduction.

BE DIRECT

This works best with people you're comfortable with personally and professionally. If you can, ask in person and then follow up with an email. Hitting people up across channels is a proven way to increase their response time—or the chances of them following up with you at all. All you really need to do is say something along the lines of, "Hey, do you know X? I'd love to talk to them about an idea I have. Would you mind making an intro?"

PROFESSIONAL COURTESY

Businesses are dependent on personal connections. For that reason, it's very common for coworkers and peers who aren't super familiar with each other to ask one another for introductions as a professional courtesy. This is especially true in current work environments, where most people have multiple positions at multiple companies throughout their career. There's a really good chance that you're fairly closely connected to anyone in the same line of work. If you work with the person you're asking a referral from, but aren't personally close, it's best to ask in person. Of course, this requires a certain degree of formality, but again, it's such a common occurrence that there's not a whole lot to worry about: "Hi [their name], have you worked with [connection name] before? I'd love to contact them about [article, project, problem they worked on]. I was hoping you could make an introduction."

"I had originally set out to expand my list of contacts and wound up with a job."

—AMAN DHESI

COLD-CALL

Generally speaking, if you're asking someone you don't know for an introduction to someone you don't know, you're better off skipping the intermediary and going straight to the source. However, affiliations can be big factors in making or breaking someone's receptivity to your request; it's the difference between, "Hi, my name's Bob," and "Hi, my name's Bob from NASA." So, if someone in your company you don't know has worked with the person you're looking to make a connection with, put in the effort. It just might keep your outreach email out of the trash bin.

Digital Etiquette for New Connections

The first rule of network building is that you're not making connections and building your network explicitly for the purpose of finding a new job; you're building a network because that's what people who enjoy successful, satisfying, and long careers do. An easy job search, or, ideally job referrals, are the by-products of a proven ability to do work, a great reputation, and an extensive, well-cultivated network of professional peers.

How to Write a Cold Introduction

While it's always better to enlist the help of someone connected to the person you'd like to connect with, there will be times when common connections don't exist. This is particularly true online. A lot of really talented people who can help advance your job search are going to be outside your existing network. To make a connection, explain your issue or idea and why you think they can help. Here is an example.

Hi _____,

I'm a copywriter at _____, and we're in the middle of a project for _____. I saw that you had delivered some stellar copy for _____ on the _____ campaign and was hoping you might be willing to talk me through some of your processes.

Would you mind spending fifteen minutes on the phone sometime that is convenient for you? I would very much appreciate it.

Cheers,

[You]

While it's best to start off with people in your personal network, your personal network is never going to match the reach, scope, and diversity of your virtual network. LinkedIn, Facebook, Twitter, and other platforms offer an amazing opportunity to amplify your job search. Connecting online is much the same as connecting offline, as far as the etiquette and process goes.

So what does that mean, specifically?

1. **Don't treat your connections like they're a means to an end.** Do that, and people will unfriend, unfollow, and disconnect from you faster than you can say "onomatopoeia." Really good networkers are innately interested in meeting people for the sake of meeting them. If that's not you, you're going to have to work on developing an intentional habit.

2. **Don't be overly familiar with new connections.** While social media can seem relaxed and unprofessional, you should still conduct yourself in the same way you would if you were in a meeting room with coworkers.

3. **Don't complain about your present job.** Referrals are based on professional respect and personal relationships. If you're belittling a boss or showing disrespect for your employers, you're basically broadcasting that you're (1) a pain in the ass to work with or (2) naïve about how to solve business problems.

4. **Don't wander off the farm.** If you're participating in an online hangout, meetup, forum, or comment section, make sure your questions and comments are relevant. Despite what you may have heard, there are some dumb questions. They are the ones that don't relate to what everyone else is talking about.

To make a good impression on new connections and in the network you're working hard to cultivate, conduct yourself like a professional. That means doing the following:

1. **Be generous with your own contacts, knowledge, and experience.** There's a term for people who are members of online groups that only participate when they need something: lurkers. If you want someone to help you, the best way is to lead by helping others.

2. **Keep it civil.** It's incredibly difficult to sniff out context and nuance in social media platforms and emails. The best way to avoid being misinterpreted is to stay neutral in your message and clear in your goals and communications and adhere to proper grammar and punctuation in your writing.

3. **Be gracious when you get turned down.** Not everyone you approach will accept your invitation to connect. It's best to simply accept their decision and move on; harassment is not a good network-building strategy. That doesn't mean you can't revisit the invitation after some time has passed and circumstances have changed.

Building Your Network

Your offline and online networks should support each other. To that end, you should make their maintenance a regular part of your work habits. But, how much is enough? The answer partly depends on your particular circumstances. The best networks grow out of personal experience. People just starting out in the workforce shouldn't worry too much about having only a few connections. However, if you've been working in a specific field for more than five years and still have only a couple dozen LinkedIn connections, you're not really networking as much as you should.

LinkedIn puts the magic number for connections at 500; that's when you really get the benefits of exponential networking and your opportunities really open up. After five years, your friends-of-friends network should have grown to the point where you can hit 500. If you're having trouble, there are a few easy and completely legitimate ways to juice your numbers.

1. **Most social networks will autopopulate your existing connections based on your email account.** Simply give the network temporary access to your email, and it will bring up accounts registered under your contacts' email addresses. You can do the same thing between social networks. For instance, if you have a lot of Facebook friends, but a small LinkedIn network, LinkedIn can suggest connections based on your Facebook account.

2. **LIONs (LinkedIn Open Networkers) are people on the service who are open to networking with anyone.** You can filter out LIONs that aren't in your industry or geographic location by entering keywords into the corresponding search filters. To do this, go the "Advanced Search" function and type "LION" into the last name field. Then, add relevant keywords in the title, company, and/or location fields. Presto, you now have a free pool of peers eager to start networking.

No matter what you do on the Internet to land a job, there will always be a human being on the other side who will make the final decision about hiring you—at least until the network becomes sentient. If you can shortcut the process and reach that person through their friends and colleagues, it's worth the effort.

In the next chapter, we'll look beyond networking and profile building toward actively searching for open positions.

How to Ask for a Job Referral

Referrals can be hugely effective in getting an interview—or the job itself. Don't be bashful about casting a wide net for referrals when you find a job opening that interests you. Coming recommended can help you stand out from the pack. Here's a sample of what to ask for.

Hi _____,

I've been thinking about making a professional move for a little while now and believe I've found a perfect next step for me. The position is _____ at _____. I've been following their work and am excited about the possibility of joining their team. I see that you worked with _____ while at _____. Would you be open to passing along my name? Any recommendation you might be willing to make on my behalf would be very much appreciated.

Many, many thanks,

[Your Name]

GET IT DONE

1. Create a list of professional contacts you know personally. Out of all the professional contacts, create a sublist of those specifically related to your career and start there. ☒ *Time on task: 1 hr.*

2. Build your LinkedIn, Facebook, and Twitter network as large as possible. Participate in job group discussions on LinkedIn and Facebook, and see if you can reach 500 connections in your first year on LinkedIn. ☒ *Time on task: 1–2 hrs weekly.*

3. Make professionally greeting new connections a habit. Write a couple of connection, introduction, and job-referral request letters. Reach out to some folks in your industry. ☒ *Time on task: 1–2 hrs weekly.*

Resources

Meetup.com

This service seeks to put meeting in-person back in social media. Users can create or find groups focused on specific interests and actually meet in the physical world. If you're serious about networking, you should definitely join the service and start attending, or even better, hosting, events.

Professional Associations

Every industry has spinoff associations that provide resources about the industry. These associations often promote events, awards, and conferences where you can make great contacts. Finding a few that are related to your career is as simple as Googling "[your industry] professional associations."

College/University Career Development Office

Having something in common with a potential employer can be a big differentiator. If you graduated college, you already have access to an existing network of professionals: your school's alumni. Reach out to your college's career development office, and see what sort of resources they can offer you.

Networking Apps

There are a bunch of different apps that put at least some of the work of networking right at your fingertips. Here are just a few of the most popular:

- Bizzabo
- Caliber
- CityHour
- Coffee the App
- Grip
- LetsLunch
- Refresh
- Weave

CHAPTER TWELVE

HAVE THEM AT HELLO

READING TIME ⧗ 30–35 MINUTES

Look Around

So, your online profile is polished, consistent across channels, and full of your best work and positive feedback from former employers. You take part in offline and online professional groups, regularly update your various social media accounts, and are an active and professional online citizen. Your professional network is growing; you have a great core group of peers, and you are generous with your own connections and experience. All the work you've done—none of which involves typing out an old-timey resume—puts you in great shape to land a position you're really excited about.

When it comes to actually applying, you want to be selective. Not every hiring manager has an identical understanding of job titles, and not all companies use particular positions in the same way. It's far better to be sure you're applying for fewer, better-suited openings than it is to apply for more, less-clear, positions. In this chapter, we'll look at the best ways to find and apply for the jobs that don't come straight to you already.

How Much Time Should You Spend on Your Job Search?

How much time you devote to seeking out new positions depends on your situation. If you're unemployed, you should treat your search like a full-time job. The more time you commit to finding a job, the more opportunities you'll uncover, and the more chances you'll make for yourself. Get up at 7 a.m., be ready to start looking by 9 a.m., take an hour off for lunch, and close up shop at 6 p.m. As a bonus, you'll already be in the workday rhythm when you find a position.

Top Job Boards and Search Sites

Indeed.com	AfterCollege.com	Vault.com
Job.com	JobShouts.com	Jobfox.com
TheLadders.com	Employment911.com	NationJob.com
Jobalot.com	Fresh-Jobs.net	JobsInPods.com
VetJobs.com	TwitJobSeek.com	SnagAJob.com
EmploymentGuide.com	Jobs.LiveCareer.com	Jobs.net
Dice.com	RealMatch.com	myCareerSpace.biz
CareerArc.com	Hirezon.com	Juju.com
CareerBuilder.com	Beyond.com	LocalHelpWanted.net
BestJobsUSA.com	JobCritters.com	Monster.com

If you already have a job but are looking to make professional moves, your best bet is to search on your own time, preferably in the morning while you're fresh, and have a few sick days or solid alibis in your back pocket for interviews. If you're set up on job boards, you receive notifications when new opportunities become available, and if you've saved your searches, then you should end up spending about the same amount of time on your search as you would browsing the news in the morning.

Passive candidates—people who are happy in their position, but could leave it if the right opportunity arises—have the easiest time maintaining a job search. If you've got a good reputation, extensive professional network, and a spotless online profile, you might already be turning down inquiries. Still, it doesn't hurt to check in with your ideal employer or wish-list company every now and again to see what they have available.

How Much Time Should You Spend on Your Job Search?

UNEMPLOYED	40 hours per week
EMPLOYED AND ACTIVELY SEARCHING	5 hours per week
EMPLOYED AND PASSIVELY SEARCHING	1 hour per week

Apply Wisely

When you're looking for a job, you want to think like a hiring manager: Filter out as much of the noise as possible. LinkedIn, Monster, Indeed, and other search tools all have something in common: they're imperfect. Even when you've typed in a specific title, location, and, if you can, salary range, it's very likely that you'll get some results for totally unsuitable openings. Some of these are going to be fairly obvious dead

Brave New Search Tools

The Internet is filled with sites that function as glorified job boards. While one prong of your attack should absolutely be scouring these resources for solid leads, there are a handful of ways that you can put the Internet to work for you. Here are a few good tools to have in your back pocket:

- GOOGLE ALERTS. Make your job search easier by automating parts of it with Google Alerts. This is a way to put Google's massive search algorithm to work for you by setting up alerts related to companies you want to work for, as well as news and trends on a particular industry, person, or company. It's very easy to set up an alert; just head to google.com/alerts and follow the instructions.

- TWELLOW. This service sorts Twitter accounts into specific categories, making it easier to locate businesses, people, and companies as part of your networking or job search. Although it's a stand-alone service, it basically recreates your Twitter network with improved search tools.

- JOB-SEARCH APPS. Along with Google Alerts and signing up for company career-page notifications, loading a few job-searching apps on your phone is a good idea. It doesn't get more convenient than jobs delivered to your pocket. In particular, JobCompass uses the GPS function of your smartphone to find positions near you, and LinkUp's job-search engine pulls only jobs that are published on a company website. While Indeed's job search can be overwhelming, it doesn't hurt to have one of the biggest job aggregators at your fingertips. Lastly, SnagAJob loads jobs by most recent posting and includes part-time and temp openings.

ducks. But there are also going to be a lot of returns that you might think to yourself, "Yeah, I *could* do that," or, "It's close enough."

If you aren't absolutely certain you're a good fit for a job, with the experience to back it up, you shouldn't even consider the position. Your time is much better spent searching for a position that you're qualified for than going through the motions for something that just isn't right.

Ideal vs. Marginal Job Openings

IDEAL	MARGINAL
Title and description matches your skills and experience	Unclear job description or one that is an imperfect match for your background
Easy commute	Requires relocation or a long commute
In-network references or connections	Completely cold application
At one of your dream companies to work for	Hard to find insight into company culture
Growth and mentorship opportunity	Lateral move or a step down in responsibility

While it might seem obvious that you shouldn't apply for jobs that aren't the right fit, you'd be amazed by how many people apply for jobs they have no business considering. "One of the main reasons I try to avoid posting openings publically on job boards and LinkedIn is that I know 60 percent to 70 percent of applications will be totally useless," notes Kelly Milner. "I mean, I had a guy apply for a senior position in marketing design and his entire work history was in plumbing pipe sales." No wonder recruiters and hiring managers give most resumes less than a 10-second look.

Recruit a Recruiter

The obvious benefit to working with recruiters is that it's their job to find you yours—and this often comes at no cost to you. And you've already developed all the tools and content you need to look attractive to employers, which are the same things you'll need to find a recruiter.

Recruiters specialize in different industries, but all fall into a few broad categories:

- Internal or corporate recruiters are full-time, staffed positions at the company they hire for. They work with HR and department heads to find the best candidate for whatever opening needs to be filled. Some keep a database of active and passive candidates on file, and it should be a goal of yours to get into that database. Once you do, any time an opening comes up, you'll have an automatic shot at being considered.

- Retained recruiters work outside of the organization that hires them and are paid a fixed fee, whether they successfully fill a position or not. Generally speaking, retained recruiters are brought in to fill senior-level positions within an organization.

- Contingency recruiters also work outside the organization that hires them, but they only get paid when they make a successful placement. This is the most common type of recruiter since they deal with all levels of placement—from college graduates to upper-management positions.

- Staffing agencies and temp recruiters supply clients with specialized employees on a short-term basis. This is a great way for job seekers to make ends meet, try out a number of work environments, and build experience quickly, but they're not so great if you want things like health insurance or any time off. That said, it's fairly common for a temp to get hired as a full-time employee by the company they've temped for.

- Consulting company recruiters work much like temp and staffing agencies except that they provide highly specialized and experienced talent. Another big difference is that these agencies will often keep paying their consultants, regardless of whether or not they are working on a project.

Finding a recruiter is a lot like finding a job: search for them online and then reach out. It takes effort to get picked up by recruiting agencies, but it can be worthwhile to develop and cultivate those relationships.

Recycle Your Best Material

Applications usually happen in one of two ways: (1) you either apply through a company's website, or (2) you send your work history and relevant information in via email. Both have advantages and disadvantages. In either case, it helps to have some items on hand to make the process more efficient. These are:

▶ An unformatted, text-only version of your work history

▶ Examples of your work in PDF, or other visual format

▶ Reference letters or referrals if you have them

▶ Any other relevant information the job posting asked for

Lucky for you, most of this material is already part of your online profile; gathering it together shouldn't be too difficult. Sometimes the application portal will be able to directly pull your information off of LinkedIn or similar online services. If that's the case, all you need to do is make sure that the right content from your profile ends up in the corresponding section of the application portal. Be ready to give the imported information a close read, though, because a lot of times the transfer of information can be buggy.

It's important to note that you don't want to cut and paste from your online profiles directly into an online job-application portal. Doing so will include a lot of information in potentially incompatible formats. In other words, when you select and copy something off the Web, there is going to be hidden information that the online portal may not know how to translate. When the portal encounters information it doesn't know what to do with, it can either stall, or altogether halt, your application or use a default translation that you're not aware of. Here's an example of what your carefully tailored LinkedIn profile may end up looking like when you cut and paste it somewhere else.

Your profile: My time at Service Management International was influenced by three major events:

▶ Rapid growth

▶ In-country legal challenges

▶ Employer's need for a flexible negotiation process

Portal translation: My time at Service Management International was influenced by major three major events¡:

- ▶ ❡ Rapid growth
- ▶ ❡ In&country legal challenges
- ▶ ❡ Employer§s need for a flexible negotiation process

Even though you have no responsibility or control over what the translation between your careful formatting and the portal's interpretation is, it's going to look like you screwed up. So, to cover your bases, keep an unformatted version of your essential information on hand when using an application portal. Most hiring managers appreciate a simple, legible version of your required documents.

Stay off the Blacklist

Hiring managers, recruiters, and employers all maintain some kind of database on who they've hired, interviewed, and considered. If you consistently apply for jobs you're not qualified for or come across as unprofessional, it will almost certainly get noted in a software program like Taleo. This also goes for overly enthusiastic (a.k.a. annoyingly repetitive) requests to connect with said hiring managers and recruiters. "If you are annoying or wasting my time by applying for everything under the sun, I'm going to make sure everyone I work with knows about it," notes Ryan Woodring. "And those notes stick around long after the people who've written them have moved on."

Beyond wasting people's time, you don't get any points for redundant material, poor writing, or simple spelling mistakes. Run the spell-checker. Take the time to read and reread your application materials closely. After all, you may get only one shot.

"Rereading reveals rubbish and redundancy."
—DUANE ALAN HAHN

Turn Your Profile into an Application

Online-application portals will often ask you to share a variety of information with them. While some of it, such as name and age, should be straightforward, other elements, depending on the employers, can be fairly novel and unexpected, such as an impromptu test related to the work you'd be performing.

Here's an example of how a typical online portal stacks up against your LinkedIn profile:

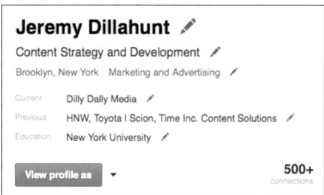

The process can get more complicated when you start filling out job-summary information, particularly since it doesn't always translate 1:1, but it's usually still pretty intuitive.

Apple Job Summary Field

LinkedIn Job Summary

Beyond transferring material from your profiles to a job-application portal, some sites like LinkedIn have made it very easy to apply for jobs by connecting you directly to the employer's job listing on its website or directly through their own sites.

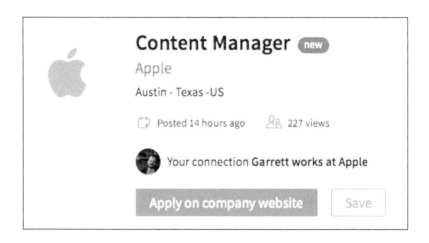

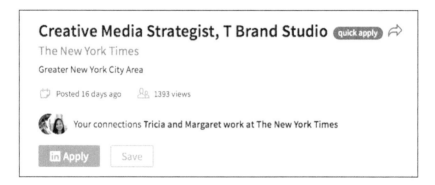

When you click the "inApply" button on LinkedIn, it takes you to this screen where you can submit your application quickly and easily. Note: A resume is optional!

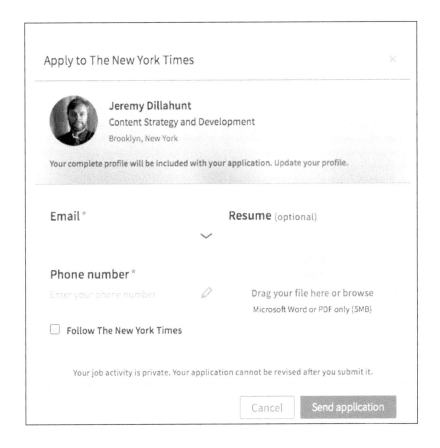

Like all good things, the inApply feature should be used with moderation. Since it reduces the application process to a couple of clicks and a few easy steps, there is a very real temptation to overuse it. But if you spam apply to a number of jobs, you run the risk of annoying the hiring manager on the receiving end. Convenience is no excuse for applying willy-nilly.

Follow Up

Just because you've sent in your application doesn't mean you can simply forget about it until someone contacts you. You always want to personalize your job application if you can. The more you can put your personality in front of the hiring managers and recruiters responsible for filling open positions, the better. But following up with an application can be tricky; you don't want to seem desperate. The rules around following up are largely determined by how personal the application experience was to begin with.

If you have had any sort of personal contact—email, phone conversation, or private message—with a real, live human at any stage in the job-application process, you need to follow up with them. It doesn't have to be much; a simple email or voice message saying, "Thanks for your help with _____ at _____," is all you need to do. Not doing so will most likely be noted as discourteous. But far more important than adhering to basic standards of etiquette, not following up means you'll miss an opportunity to deepen the discussion about your application—many hiring managers and recruiters expect it.

For applications that came through a referral, it's essential that you follow up with both the person who gave the referral and the hiring manager. Using a group email will reinforce the common connection and open up the opportunity for a more nuanced dialogue between you, the hiring manager, and your contact.

As far as when to follow up, don't let more than 24 hours pass. If you don't hear back within a week, it's acceptable to send another follow-up. But two is the limit; any more and you could come across as impatient or pushy.

How to Export Your LinkedIn Profile as a Traditional Resume

Now, I know what you're thinking. We've gone to great pains and lengths throughout this book to move your job-seeking strategy out of the dark ages and into something that's more social, natural, and effective. The sad truth of the matter is that, unfortunately, some gatekeepers will insist on seeing a traditional resume, which leaves you with two options: (1) don't provide one or don't apply, which pretty much counts you out of the race before it starts, or (2) bend to the will of whatever fossil is sitting at the hiring desk, and give him or her a resume.

Since option one is a pretty good way to remain perpetually unemployed, you may, in some instances, need a traditional resume. Thankfully, you don't actually need to type out and format two boring pages on your own. LinkedIn has your back. It offers a resume builder, a quick and easy process that converts your profile into a resume document, as if by magic. To get your resume, just follow these steps:

STEP 1: Go to resume.linkedinlabs.com.

STEP 2: Allow the program to access your profile.

Grant Resume Builder access to your LinkedIn Account "Jeremy Dillahunt"
On Feb 17 you granted Resume Builder permission to use your LinkedIn Account.

In about a second, the information in your profile will populate a traditional-looking resume, with a variety of template options. You can then download or print a PDF version of the file. LinkedIn will also provide you with a URL so you can share your new resume on your various online channels. You can set privacy settings around who can see your resume—only you, your connections, everyone, and so on—and you can create, edit, share, and manage multiple resumes for tailored job applications.

GET IT DONE

Applying for a job is fairly straightforward, but online portals are adding a layer of technology that can make the process a bit more complex. To make the procedure more efficient and less prone to mistakes, you should:

1. Determine how much time you should put into searching. Then, commit to a regular search schedule. ⊠ *Time on task: 1–40 hrs per week.*

2. Set up Google Alerts, and load your phone with whichever job-search tools might make the job search work best for you. ⊠ *Time on task: 30 mins–1 hr.*

3. Put some time into researching recruiters and temp agencies in your area. If you can get in with them, it may help you get your foot in the door at a company on your shortlist, particularly if you're new to the labor market. ⊠ *Time on task: 1–3 hrs.*

4. Once you've identified some ideal openings, start applying. Reuse the best parts of your profiles, tailor pain letters to employer needs, and, if, God forbid you need a resume, just export one from your LinkedIn profile. Remember, nobody likes a spammer, so make sure the jobs you go for actually match your background and experience. ⊠ *Time on task: 1 hr per application.*

Resources

Experience Works Online Practice Application

www.experienceworks.org/site/PageServer?pagename= Practice_Online_application

Don't be put off by this organization's focus on helping older job seekers navigate the hiring process. Their sample online-application template is one of the better ones available. It'll take you through the steps you'll take when applying online, as well as give you an idea of what sort of information you should have prepared.

Job-Applications.com

This site hosts thousands of application forms from common employers—from Walmart to CVS—that you can download and fill out beforehand. This is a great option for making sure that your applications are free of spelling and grammar mistakes before you submit them. It will also save you time and make the process more efficient.

FindARecruiter.com

This is a pretty good place to start looking for recruiters. The database is pretty robust, and most sites it links to are active. While there are not very many search options available on the site, it is a useful jumping-off point if you're interested in pursuing the recruiter route.

PDF Converters

PDFs are a very common document file, and almost all online application portals can accept them. A bunch of different online services offer free document conversions. If you don't know how to do this on your own or don't have the right software installed, Google "PDF converter" and upload your work history, references, job summaries, and any other documents you have.

ApplyMate.com

This free service will help you keep track of your applications by segmenting the individual applications in stages of the process. You can see where you've applied to, if you've heard anything back, when you applied, and a bunch of other details that are easy to forget.

CHAPTER THIRTEEN

CLOSE THE DEAL

READING TIME ⧗ 30–40 MINUTES

You Got This

Standing between a mountain of applications and you actually being employed, there is still one final stage. Up until this point you've been polishing your work history, cultivating contacts, developing a professional reputation through your online channels, and researching and applying for jobs you know you can do. It would be a shame to let all that work go to waste by being unprepared for arguably the most important moment of the job hunt: face-to-face impressions.

The good news is that your online profile and reputation have paved the way for what will hopefully be a comfortable, relaxed interview session. Whoever is sitting on the opposite side of the table will no doubt have browsed your work history, references, job summaries, and social media channels—and, of course, Googled you. Since you've already curated an impressive bunch of content—they already know you can do the job—this next stage is simply a matter of reinforcing those expectations—and exceeding them.

With all the work you've done developing your online profile, you should be confident in the knowledge that your job interviewers are predisposed to seeing you in a good light. To be frank, you wouldn't be called in for an interview if a recruiter or potential employer didn't see promise in your ability to add value to their company and do the job in question. So, when you walk into that conference room, coffee shop, or office, all you really need to do is build on what they already know about you.

Let's quickly cover the basics of what they'll know and what they'll base their questions on.

WORK HISTORY

One of the most basic components of an interview is fleshing out the details of the job summaries you've shared on your application and your online profiles. An interviewer will be looking for two things: examples of your day-to-day responsibilities and inconsistencies in what you say in person and what you've written down.

"It's amazing how many people contradict themselves in interviews," notes Ryan Woodring. "You'd think this was basic but, in my experience, it's not." By checking to see if your work history is consistent with what you claim, a potential employer is just doing due diligence. So keep your story straight.

On the other side of the coin, the person interviewing you is going to be digging for specific examples of challenges you encountered on the job and solutions you created to overcome them. It can't be overstated how important it is to have a few anecdotes ready to share. A few pretty standard areas that regularly come up in interviews are leadership, mentoring, difficult clients, revenue growth, efficiencies, strategy, products, and business development. Of course, this is by no means a comprehensive list of what a potential employer may ask about. Your particular circumstances, expertise, and industry will shape the interview's specifics.

WORK SAMPLES

Providing examples of your work is a must during any interview. If you're not asked to provide any, bring them anyway. While you might not end up using them, it's better to have them on hand than not to. At a very basic level, examples of your work serve as evidence to back up the claims you've made in your job summaries. It's a way for potential employers to concretely understand what you've abstractly described in your job descriptions. The great thing about work examples is that you're going to be bringing only the best of what you've worked on. This will help quickly establish that you're a valuable and experienced potential hire.

As with your work summaries, you should expect to be asked to talk in detail about the examples you bring in. Topics like what the budget was, what the project's deadline and time frame were, what role you played in the team that executed the work, and what specific work you performed are all fair game. One quick note here: It is really important to be specific and honest about your role. "I've seen a lot of instances in which it's clear that the work was a team effort yet the person is omitting that fact," says Sarah El Batanouny. "Don't take credit for everything if you were actually part of a team."

FIRST IMPRESSIONS

Your online profiles will have created an impression about what sort of person you are in the minds of the people interviewing you. While you can hope to influence their take, you can't expect to control it. When you make that first, physical contact, you'll have a brief opportunity to reinforce the reputation you've presented online. How brief? According to several studies, only seven seconds. That's a pretty small window. Make sure you don't yawn, smell bad, or have a bit of toast stuck on your collar. The vast majority of the time it's best to shoot for professional, likable, and polite. You can do that simply by smiling, offering your hand for a shake, and letting them know you're excited for the opportunity and happy to meet them. Starting an interview with no marks against you means you'll have an easier time focusing on developing a positive experience for both you and the interviewer.

One of the big things people look for in interviews is whether or not you'll be a good fit for the company's culture. Some companies, like Zappos, are infamous for their relaxed nature, while others, such as Morgan Stanley, are known for their strict adherence to social protocols. You could be the most qualified, experienced, knowledgeable candidate for a job, but if you don't "fit in," you'll probably be passed over.

A word about business culture: there's no point in trying to fake who you are in order to get a job. If you're not a natural fit for an organization, odds are you'll be a miserable employee looking for a new job soon after you start.

Anticipating, thinking about, and developing a strategy around the questions you'll be asked is an essential part of good interview preparation. The next step is getting yourself in the right frame of mind for the interview itself.

> "I had a job interview at an insurance company once and the lady said, 'Where do you see yourself in five years?' and I said 'Celebrating the fifth-year anniversary of you asking me this question.'"
> —MITCH HEDBERG

Interview Strategies

If the thought of having to prove yourself to perfect strangers makes you uncomfortable, don't worry; you're not alone. Almost everyone, interviewers included, get nervous before an in-person meeting. It's natural to get the jitters when you're meeting someone new, especially someone who has the power to make or break your chances for a new job. Planning ahead, visualizing, doing controlled breathing exercises, and any number of other practices are great ways to manage preinterview anxiety.

Visualize yourself creating a strong impression of how you will benefit the employer. "You'd be surprised at how many people don't understand this basic fact," says Ryan Woodring. "You're not called into an interview to talk about yourself. You're there to talk about how you will make the company better in a demonstrable, proven way." Let's just call it the golden rule of interviewing: it's not about you; it's about how you will help the company.

Everybody has rituals they perform before a job interview, and you should, too. Just like professional athletes will use the same routine, year in and year out, to get ready for a big game, you need a way to get your mind in "the zone." All of these prep rituals share a common goal: to promote focus, clarity, and confidence. Here are a few basics to consider adding to your preinterview preparation routine.

- **Get a good night's sleep.** A bad night's sleep can make it look like you've got a hangover, will slow down your thinking, and, no surprises here, can make it seem like you're tired. None of these is a good impression to make.

- **Don't drink alcohol two days beforehand.** Drinking alcohol can make it more difficult to get a good night's sleep and will affect the way you look: puffy eyes, swollen face, red eyes, and so on. Just abstain leading up to any interview.

- **Exercise leading up to the interview.** Regular exercise helps reduce stress, work out anxiety, and minimize nervousness. It will also help you get a good night's sleep and improve your mental acuity.

- **Eat light before the interview.** A heavy meal before bed will interrupt a good night's sleep and thus slow down your thinking. Also, you don't want to be dealing with indigestion or gas while trying to make a good impression. Avoid big, rich, heavy meals for 48 hours before your interview.

- **Arrive early.** Cutting an interview close can mean showing up sweaty, out of breath, or disheveled. You want to get to where you're going with at least 30 minutes to spare. Take this time to familiarize yourself with the check-in protocols and layout of the interview location—and give yourself a few minutes to calm down.

- **Practice controlled breathing.** Meditating has been proven to help with focus and to calm anxiety. Before any interview, it's a good idea to spend a few minutes controlling your breathing and clearing your mind of everything that's competing for your attention.

All of these things will put you in a great position to perform well during your interview.

The Five Secrets of Job-Interview Success

If you go into an interview with a clear idea of what you want a potential employer to remember about you, you'll have a better chance at succeeding than if you go in without a plan. Follow these five steps to ace the interview.

1. RESEARCH

Once you've been invited to interview, you'll want to double down on any research that you've already done related to the company, the job, and who you'll be interviewing with. Whether it's through email, over the phone, or through a professional network's private messaging system, someone is going to coordinate your interview schedule. Ask that person who you'll be interviewing with. Most times, they'll let you know, and you can begin researching with specific people in mind. Research is important because it helps differentiate basic answers from nuanced, informed ones.

2. PREPARE YOURSELF

You can't prepare yourself enough for a job interview. Take the research you've found and mold it to the points you want to make during the interview. Bring in pie charts, add a multimedia component to your presentation, bake cookies, buy a new suit, or create collateral for your interviewers to take with them. If you really, really want the job, there's no good reason not to go all out during the interview.

3. BUILD A NARRATIVE

Interviews are the ideal opportunity to talk about what you've been working toward. Once you've established your ability to do the job, potential employers want to know where you see yourself in the future. As with any story worth telling, what you've done has to lead in to what you plan on doing. Take another look at chapter 5, and then build a narrative that reflects your experience, failures, and successes and includes how you can really add value to your potential employer's business. Do this in specific, relevant ways directly related to your work history.

Your narrative should be broken up into three parts: a beginning, middle, and next act. Each part should correspond to a specific moment in your work history or specific examples of your work. Open with what attracted you to your line of work in the first place. Then discuss how you've grown—say, how a project opened up your understanding to new, untapped business opportunities. And finally, talk about the future and what you want to build with the knowledge you have. As long as you're not spouting rock-star fantasies, nobody is going to penalize you for exhibiting ambition and vision.

4. REHEARSE

You can have the greatest idea in the world, but if you don't have a good pitch, no one's going to listen to you. Rehearsing the points you want your interviewers to take home with them isn't just a good idea; it's critical.

Interviews are a mix of the personal and the professional. You may start by answering a question about a specific problem the company is facing and end up on what is was like when you went to Mexico for Christmas vacation. A rambling conversation is a natural by-product of almost all "get to know each other" meetings.

What you want to rehearse for are the moments that you can tie your conversation back to a point or example that are important for you to make. If you want your interview to be a success, focus on three key points that will help the business in whatever way the role you're interviewing for requires.

5. ASK THE FINAL QUESTION

At the end of every interview, there's an opening when the interviewer will say, "I think that about covers it, and I want to be sensitive to your time constraints; is there anything else you want to ask?" This is an opportunity that a lot of job seekers miss. Essentially, the door's wide open for you to bring everything into focus by replying, "Yes. I'm curious to know if I've said anything or given you any reason to believe I'm not a good fit for the job?"

Asking direct questions like this is a great way to turn the tables on the interviewer and establish that you're unafraid of honest, pointed feedback. Basically, what happens is you turn a conceptual exercise into a real-work scenario. The interviewer gets the opportunity to see how you handle a critique, and you get a second chance to explain an answer that the interviewer might not have been satisfied with. It will also give you really good insight into what to address in your follow-up email.

Follow Up

As with a job reference or an application to a company where you have a personal connection, it's essential that you follow up after an interview. The most important part about following up is expressing your gratitude for being considered for the job. As we discussed earlier, you obviously don't want to sound desperate. Just convey that you're excited about the opportunity to work somewhere you've always respected.

Beyond common courtesy, a follow-up is your chance to address any point you may have forgotten to make or explained poorly, or just to reinforce the message that you want your interviewers to remember. "A thank-you note is always a good idea," says Sarah El Batanouny. "It's an expected professional courtesy."

An email the day after the interview is a good way to remind your potential employer of your strengths. Your specific points may get lost, while the courtesy is remembered, and that's fine. You can create a more memorable impression by bucking the status quo and choosing a less familiar way of saying, "Thanks." A short handwritten note is one option. Snail mail has quickly fallen to the realm of novelty in the face of so many electronic alternatives, and so it's a memorable alternative.

Whatever route you choose, just don't send gifts; they can come across as bribes.

You're Worth It

If all goes well and you nail your interview, the end of any job search is a salary negotiation. Any business worth its reputation will offer you lower than what they're prepared to part with. So, be prepared to fight not just for what's appropriate for the position, but for what you're worth.

Finding out what a fair salary is for any given position is pretty easy these days. LinkedIn offers salary range as part of its value-add for premium accounts, and several databases track self-reported ranges. In the current work environment, it's less of a taboo to discuss what you make than it was even ten years ago. While most companies frown on employees sharing salary information, you have to understand that it's less about rules than it is about maintaining an edge during negotiations: if one party has more information than the other, it stands to reason that they will benefit more. To find out the baseline salary for the job you're applying for, do this:

▶ Google the job title and "salary range."

▶ Research the salary range online.

▶ Ask on your professional networks.

▶ Ask your personal connections at work.

The baseline, however, is just the baseline. You'll want to use what you find as a starting point and add your own personal value on top of that. The best way to do this is to write it all down; that way, you have that info on hand as backup during negotiations.

The Five Secrets of Salary Negotiation

Negotiations can be stressful, but you'll be best served, both in compensation and in the respect you'll establish, by not taking what's on the table. Here are five strategies to consider.

I. RESEARCH

Just as you would provide a client with a breakdown of costs associated with a service or product, you'll want to give the person you're negotiating with a fact-based breakdown of the reasons for your ask. You can do this by referencing the databases I mentioned earlier, and by anecdotally relaying the answers you received from professional peers. Don't use their names, though.

2. MAKE YOUR CASE

There's a reason they made you the offer; they think you're the best candidate. Best candidates shouldn't get average salaries. Remind them of all the reasons why you're the one: the experience you have, the vision you're bringing, and, when applicable, the amount of revenue you'll bring in or save.

3. PERSONALLY APPEAL

Both you and the person hiring you know that you're just looking for a fair and equitable agreement. Bringing up the fact that your negotiating counterpart would do the same is a fair play.

4. OFFER A RANGE

A good way to test whether you're in the ballpark or not is to add 15 percent to 30 percent to whatever your last salary was. If you were making $100,000 at your last job, let your negotiating partner know that you'd be comfortable in the $115,000 to $130,000 range. Most likely you'll land somewhere in the middle.

5. JUST ASK

One of the most effective salary-negotiation techniques is to simply ask for what you want and make your new employer show their cards as to why they think it's too high. Once you've got their arguments out in the open, you can refute them. They might just agree to your request, for expediency's sake.

Interviewing is the last step in the long process of landing your next job. If you've made it this far, you're already qualified. Even if you don't get the first job you're invited to interview for, know that you're doing a lot of things right and are on the right track.

GET IT DONE

1. You got this. Look back through all of the material you've put online to create that ideal version of yourself. Be confident. Do whatever it takes to get yourself in the right state of mind. ⏲ *Time on task: 1 hr.*

2. Take care of yourself. Get a good night's sleep, hold off on the booze, and burn of some of the jitters with a bit of exercise. ⏲ *Time on task: 1 hr.*

3. Do your homework. Research the role, company, and people who will be interviewing you in greater depth. Pull together relevant work samples. Research salary levels, and come prepared with evidence to support whatever pay grade you're hoping to hit. ⏲ *Time on task: 1–3 hrs.*

Resources

Payscale.com

This service will advise you on what the average salary is for your title, as well as other considerations useful for convincing your potential employer that you're worth the asking price.

What to Wear to a Job Interview by Liz Ryan

www.forbes.com/sites/lizryan/2015/03/21/what-to-wear-to-a
-job-interview/#4ffe3a837605

Liz Ryan is a former recruiter with an entire career's worth of advice on everything from how to impress in a cover letter to negotiating a salary. In this two-minute video for *Forbes* magazine, she covers the basics of how to present yourself for the big day.

Five Energizing Songs to Pump You Up Before Your Interview, and Possibly Get You the Job

http://thoughtcatalog.com/danny-murphy/2015/03/5-energizing
-songs-to-pump-you-up-before-your-interview-and-possibly-get
-you-the-job

Thought Catalog put together an energizing selection of tunes to listen to before heading in to meet your potential employers. It might be a bit silly, but every little bit can help. Get pumped!

CONCLUSION

FROM HERE ON

So here we are, at the end. While it's been a lot of work, by now, you should be in a better position to develop a long, successful career and navigate the numerous job changes that will almost inevitably be part of your working life. Make no mistake about it: the work world is changing more rapidly now than ever, and it's very likely that the next 20 years will see even more fundamental changes. Thankfully, all the hard work you've put into your online channels over the course of this book set you up to succeed; by adapting now, you'll be in a better position to take advantage of whatever changes ultimately come.

In all likelihood, more Americans will be working as freelancers in the near future. Some studies estimate as much as 50 percent of the country's workforce will be making most of their money through the "gig economy." As a freelancer, you can expect to change jobs every six months (since the government requires that any longer continuous employment be full time). Unless my math is off, that means workers might hold as many as 100 "gigs" throughout their careers. While that scenario is probably extreme, even a small step in that direction means that the strategies, processes, and habits I've outlined in this book will be more relevant than ever.

Change is difficult for everyone. Our brains aren't wired for it, and our social structures still favor continuity over disruption. The problem is that our economy, particularly as it relates to the workforce, changes all the time. If it feels like a difficult act to balance, it's no fault of your own. Change brings stress, even when it's a positive change.

The good news is that you've already laid the groundwork for a process that will automatically absorb much of the stress and work that goes into building a long-term career. Your professional network will keep you abreast of changes and trends affecting your industry. And growing your connections can provide you with a steady stream of opportunities. Your online profile will establish your expertise in the eyes of future employers, and your good digital citizenship will advance your sterling reputation into yet unknown and unconnected professional networks.

Looking for a job that does more than pay the bills can be frustrating. There are so many moving parts to take into account, from the people you work with to changes in direction handed down from senior management. When you do hit turbulence, it's important to stay patient, be flexible, and keep your options open—all strategies that, after reading this book, you're doing already.

It's been said that good things come to those who wait. But they also come to those who work for it. With all the work you've done now, you shouldn't have to wait too long.

REFERENCES

Adams, Susan. "4 Ways to Use Facebook to Find a Job." *Forbes.* February 6, 2014. www.forbes.com/sites/susanadams/2014 /02/06/4-ways-to-use-facebook-to-find-a-job/#54d6d4537ce3.

Adams, Susan. "The 10 Skills Employers Most Want in 20-Something Employees." *Forbes.* Accessed October 11, 2013. www.forbes.com /sites/susanadams/2013/10/11/the-10-skills-employers-most -want-in-20-something-employees.

Adams, Tim. "The Interview: Robert Pirsig." *The Guardian.* November 18, 2006. www.theguardian.com/books/2006 /nov/19/fiction.

Andrews, Paul W., and Thomson, J. Anderson, Jr. "Depression's Evolutionary Roots." *Scientific American.* August 25, 2009. www.scientificamerican.com/article/depressions-evolutionary.

Bakker, Lotte. "Engagement on Global Facebook Career Pages Increased by 32 percent in the Last Twelve Months." Maximum, Social Recruitment Monitor. October 14, 2013. www.socialrecruitmentmonitor.com/blog/engagement-on -global-facebook-career-pages-increased-by-32.

Bersin, Josh. "Corporate Recruiting Explodes: A New Breed of Service Providers." *Forbes.* May 23, 2013. www.forbes.com/sites/joshbersin /2013/05/23/corporate-recruitment-transformed-new-breed-of -service-providers.

Bullas, Jeff. "23 Epic Twitter Facts and Statistics That May Surprise You." JeffBullas.com. April 25, 2015. www.jeffbullas.com/2015 /04/25/23-epic-twitter-facts-and-statistics-that-may-surprise-you.

Bureau of Labor Statistics. "Economic News Release: Job Openings and Labor Turnover Summary." Accessed February 9, 2016. www.bls.gov/news.release/jolts.nr0.htm.

Bureau of Labor Statistics. "News Release: Job Openings and Labor Turnover—December 2015." Accessed February 9, 2016. www.bls.gov/news.release/pdf/jolts.pdf.

CareerBuilder.com. "Seventy-Five Percent of Workers Who Applied to Jobs through Various Venues in the Last Year Didn't Hear Back from Employers, CareerBuilder Survey Finds." Accessed February 22, 2016. www.careerbuilder.com/share/aboutus /pressreleasesdetail.aspx?sd=2%2F20%2F2013&id=pr740&ed =12%2F31%2F2013.

CareerCast.com. "The Most Stressful Jobs of 2015." Accessed February 22, 2016. www.careercast.com/jobs-rated/most-stressful-jobs-2015.

Cenedella, Marc. "Leonardo da Vinci's Resume." TheLadders.com. Accessed February 22, 2016. www.theladders.com/career -newsletters/leonardo-da-vinci-resume.

Crotty, James Marshall. "60% of College Grads Can't Find Work in Their Field. Is a Management Degree the Answer?" *Forbes*. March 1, 2012. www.forbes.com/sites/jamesmarshallcrotty/2012 /03/01/most-college-grads-cant-find-work-in-their-field-is-a -management-degree-the-answer.

Cruz, Esther. "4 Trends That Will Define Recruiting in the US in 2015." *LinkedIn Talent Blog*. Accessed October 30, 2014. business.linkedin .com/talent-solutions/blog/2014/10/4-trends-that-will-define -recruiting-in-the-us-in-2015.

Davidson, Jacob. "The 7 Social Media Mistakes Most Likely to Cost You a Job." *Time*. October 16, 2014. time.com/money/3510967 /jobvite-social-media-profiles-job-applicants.

Davies, Jay. "If You Want a Better Job, Ditch Your Resume." *Huffington Post.* September 1, 2015. www.huffingtonpost.com /hippo-reads/if-you-want-a-better-job-ditch-your-resume_b _8066050.html?utm_hp_ref=business&ir=Business.

Desilver, Drew. "5 Facts About Today's College Graduates." Pew Research Center, Fact Tank. May 30, 2014. www.pewresearch.org /fact-tank/2014/05/30/5-facts-about-todays-college-graduates.

Edunov, Sergey, et al., "Three and a Half Degrees of Separation." Research at Facebook. Accessed February 22, 2016. research.facebook.com/blog/three-and-a-half-degrees -of-separation.

Erickson, Robin. "Benchmarking Talent Acquisition: Increasing Spend, Cost Per Hire, and Time to Fill." Bersin by Deloitte. April 23, 2015. www.bersin.com/blog/post/Benchmarking-Talent-Acquisition -Increasing-Spend2c-Cost-Per-Hire2c-and-Time-to-Fill.aspx.

Experience, Inc. "Career Statistics." Accessed February 22, 2016. www.experience.com/alumnus/article?channel_id=career _management&source_page=additional_articles&article _id=article_1247505066959.

Fahey, Mark. "Twitter's Cash Puts It in a League of Its Own." CNBC, The Big Crunch. January 28, 2016. www.cnbc.com/2016/01/28 /twitters-cash-puts-it-in-a-league-of-its-own.html.

Francis, David R. "Employers' Replies to Racial Names." The National Bureau of Economic Research. Accessed February 22, 2016. www.nber.org/digest/sep03/w9873.html.

Guarini, Drew. "'Marijuana Dealer and Nefarious Dude' Resume Makes the Rounds." *Huffington Post.* October 5, 2012. www.huffingtonpost.com/2012/10/05/marijuana-dealer -nefarious-dude-resume_n_1943189.html.

Harris, Peter. "Why Only 2% of Applicants Actually Get Interviews." Workopolis.com. Accessed December 1, 2015. careers.workopolis .com/advice/only-2-of-applicants-actually-get-interviews-heres -how-to-be-one-of-them.

Hayes, Phillip. "Kloodle and Ofsted—How to Evidence Your Students' Employability Progression." *Kloodle Blog*. Accessed November 26, 2015. blog.kloodle.com/2015/11/kloodle-and-ofsted.

Internet Live Stats. "Internet Users." Accessed February 22, 2016. www.internetlivestats.com/internet-users.

Internet Live Stats, "Internet Users by Country (2014)." Accessed February 22, 2016. www.internetlivestats.com/internet-users -by-country.

InterviewSuccessFormula.com. "The Job Search Today." Accessed February 22, 2016. www.interviewsuccessformula.com/ISF -JobSearchToday972.png.

Joyce, Susan P. "What 80 Percent of Employers Do Before Inviting You for an Interview." *Huffington Post*. March 1, 2014. www.huffingtonpost.com/susan-p-joyce/job-search-tips _b_4834361.html.

Kahneman, Daniel. *Thinking, Fast and Slow*. New York: Farrar, Strauss and Giroux, 2011.

Kaputa, Catherine. *You Are a Brand!* London: Nicholas Brealey Publishing, 2012.

Kaufman, Micha. "Five Reasons Half of You Will Be Freelancers in 2020." *Forbes*. February 28, 2014. www.forbes.com/sites /michakaufman/2014/02/28/five-reasons-half-of-you-will -be-freelancers-in-2020/#237a48d67300.

King, Rachel. "LinkedIn Surpasses 300 Million Users, Wants 3.3 Billion." *ZDNet*. April 18, 2014. www.zdnet.com/article /linkedin-surpasses-300-million-users-wants-3-3-billion.

Knowledge@Wharton. "Why the Job Search Is Like 'Throwing Paper Airplanes into the Galaxy.'" February 29, 2012. knowledge.wharton .upenn.edu/article/why-the-job-search-is-like-throwing-paper -airplanes-into-the-galaxy.

LePage, Evan. "A Long List of Instagram Statistics and Facts (That Prove Its Importance)." September 17, 2015. blog.hootsuite.com /instagram-statistics-for-business.

Levenson, Larry. "25 LinkedIn Facts and Statistics for 2015." *Sensible Marketing Blog.* March 20, 2015. www.sensiblemarketing.com /blog/25-linkedin-facts-and-statistics-for-2015

Mayo Clinic. "Meditation: A Simple, Fast Way to Reduce Stress." July 19, 2014. www.mayoclinic.org/tests-procedures/meditation /in-depth/meditation/art-20045858.

McCue, T. J. "Facebook Has 40 Million-Plus Small Business Pages." *Forbes.* April 30, 2015. www.forbes.com/sites/tjmccue/2015/04/30 /facebook-has-40-million-plus-small-business-pages/#5b64457d2aa1.

Medved, J. P. "Top 15 Recruiting Statistics for 2014." *Capterra Talent Management Blog.* February 20th, 2014. blog.capterra.com /top-15-recruiting-statistics-2014.

Messieh, Nancy. "43 percent of All LinkedIn Users Are in the US, IBM Is the Company with the Most Followers." *TNW News.* February 25, 2012.thenextweb.com/socialmedia/2012/02/25 /43-of-all-linkedin-users-are-in-the-us-ibm-is-the-company -with-the-most-followers/#gref.

Noyes, Dan. "The Top 20 Valuable Facebook Statistics—Updated December 2015." Zephoria Digital Marketing. December 31, 2015. zephoria.com/top-15-valuable-facebook-statistics.

Palfrey, John, and Gassner, Urs. *Born Digital.* New York: Basic Books, 2008.

Park, Lorene D. "Social Media and Employment Law— Are Courts Catching Up?" Wolters Kluwer. May 14, 2015. www.employmentlawdaily.com/index.php/2015/05/14 /social-media-and-employment-law-are-courts-catching-up.

Parrack, Dave. "10 Reasons Why People Still Use Facebook." Makeuseof.com. July 16, 2014. www.makeuseof.com/tag /10-reasons-people-still-use-facebook-ask-results.

Pitts, Anna. "You Only Have 7 Seconds to Make a Strong First Impression." *Business Insider.* April 8, 2013. www.businessinsider.com/only-7-seconds-to-make-first-impression-2013-4.

Prensky, Marc. "Digital Natives, Digital Immigrants." *On the Horizon* 9, no. 5 (October 2001).

Restle, Hope. "Here's Who Is Using Twitter around the World." *Business Insider.* June 30, 2015. www.businessinsider.com/who-uses-twitter-2015-6.

Rossheim, John. "Mobile Recruiting Trends: A Better Candidate Experience." Monster.com. Accessed February 22, 2016. hiring.monster.com/hr/hr-best-practices/recruiting-hiring-advice/attracting-job-candidates/mobile-recruiting-trends.aspx.

Ryan, Liz. "How to Write Your Human-Voiced Resume." *Forbes.* July 17, 2014. www.forbes.com/sites/lizryan/2014/07/17/how-to-write-your-human-voiced-resume/2.

Ryan, Liz. "The Horrible Truth about Online Job Applications." *Forbes.* November 21, 2014. www.forbes.com/sites/lizryan/2014/11/21/the-horrible-truth-about-online-job-applications/2.

Sebastian, Michael. "Content Marketing Now Comprises 40 percent of LinkedIn's Ad Revenue." *Ad Age.* April 30, 2015. adage.com/article/digital/content-marketing-comprises-40-linkedin-s-ad-revenue/298375.

Share, Jacob. "150 Funniest Resume Mistakes, Bloopers, and Blunders Ever." JobMob. Accessed February 22, 2016. jobmob.co.il/blog/funniest-resume-mistakes.

Shaw, Charlie. "37 Employers Share the Most Cringe-Worthy Resume or Job Application They've Ever Seen." Thought Catalog. February 26, 2014. thoughtcatalog.com/charlie-shaw/2014/02/37-employers-share-the-most-cringeworthy-resume-or-job-application-theyve-ever-seen.

Smith, Craig. "By the Numbers: 90 Amazing Facebook Page Statistics." DMR. January 27, 2016. expandedramblings.com/index.php /facebook-page-statistics.

Smith, Craig. "By the Numbers: 125+ Amazing LinkedIn Statistics." DMR. December 15, 2015. expandedramblings.com/index.php /by-the-numbers-a-few-important-linkedin-stats.

Smith, Jacquelyn. "14 Tips for Staying Calm during a Job Interview." *Forbes.* March 26, 2013. www.forbes.com/sites/jacquelynsmith /2013/03/26/14-tips-for-staying-calm-during-a-job-interview /#5f338d652c48.

Smooke, David. "Marketo says, '80 Candidates: 8 Interviews: 1 Hire.'" *SmartRecruiters Blog.* February 13, 2013. www.smartrecruiters .com/blog/marketo-says-80-candidates-8-interviews-1-hire.

Society for Human Resource Management. "Time to Fill." Accessed February 29, 2016. www.shrm.org/research/articles/articles /pages/metricofthemonthtimetofill.aspx.

Statista, "Cumulative Total of Tumblr Blogs Between May 2011 and January 2016 (in millions)." Accessed February 22, 2016. www.statista.com/statistics/256235/total-cumulative-number -of-tumblr-blogs.

Statista. "Number of Facebook Users in the United States as of January 2015, by Age Group (in millions)." Accessed February 22, 2016. www.statista.com/statistics/398136/us-facebook-user -age-groups.

Statista. "Number of Monthly Active Twitter Users Worldwide from 1st Quarter 2010 to 4th Quarter 2015 (in millions)." Accessed February 22, 2016. www.statista.com/statistics/282087 /number-of-monthly-active-twitter-users.

Stephens, Mark Michael. "Squarespace: How to Grow a Company from $30k to $38M." *Alley Watch.* May 29, 2014. www.alleywatch .com/2014/05/squarespace-how-to-grow-a-company-from -30k-to-38m.

Stynes, Tess. "USA Today Top U.S. Newspaper in Total Circulation." *Wall Street Journal.* May 1 2014.

Thayer, Colette. "Protecting Older Workers Against Discrimination Act (POWADA) Public Opinion Report." AARP Research. May 2012. www.aarp.org/research/topics/economics/info-2014/POWADA.html.

Wall Street Journal. "Self Service Classified Ads." Accessed February 22, 2016. classifieds.wsj.com/ad/GetEstimate.jsp.

Weber, Lauren. "Your Resume vs. Oblivion." *Wall Street Journal.* January 24, 2012. www.wsj.com/articles/SB1000142405297020462 4204577178941034941330.

INDEX

CPSIA information can be obtained
at www.ICGtesting.com
Printed in the USA
BVOW11s0322170416

444429BV00005B/5/P